PRACTICAL SOCIAL WORK

Series Editor: Jo Campling

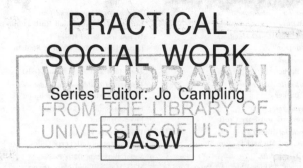

BASW

Editorial Advisory Board:
Robert Adams, Terry Bamford, Charles Barker,
Lena Dominelli, Malcolm Payne, Michael Preston-Shoot,
Daphne Statham and Jane Tunstill

Social work is at an important stage in its development. All professions must be responsive to changing social and economic conditions if they are to meet the needs of those they serve. This series focuses on sound practice and the specific contributions which social workers can make to the well-being of our society.

The British Association of Social Workers has always been conscious of its role in setting guidelines for practice and in seeking to raise professional standards. The conception of the Practical Social Work series arose from a survey of BASW members to discover where they, the practitioners in social work, felt there was the most need for new literature. The response was overwhelming and enthusiastic, and the result is a carefully planned, coherent series of books. The emphasis is firmly on practice set in a theoretical framework. The books will inform, stimulate and promote discussion, thus adding to the further development of skills and high professional standards. All the authors are practitioners and teachers of social work representing a wide variety of experience.

JO CAMPLING

A list of published f

D0412294

PRACTICAL SOCIAL WORK

Social Work and Empowerment
Robert Adams

Social Work and Mental Handicap
David Anderson

Beyond Casework
James G. Barber

Social Work with Addictions
James G. Barber

Citizen Involvement
Peter Beresford and Suzy Croft

Practising Social Work Law
Suzy Braye and Michael Preston-Shoot

Social Workers at Risk
Robert Brown, Stanley Bute and Peter Ford

Social Workers and Mental Illness
Alan Butler and Colin Pritchard

Social Work and Europe
Crescy Cannan, Lynn Berry and
Karen Lyons

Residential Work
Roger Clough

Social Work and Child Abuse
David M. Cooper and David Ball

Management in Social Work
Veronica Coulshed

Social Work Practice
Veronica Coulshed

Social Work and Local Politics
Paul Daniel and John Wheeler

Sociology in Social Work Practice
Peter R. Day

Anti-Racist Social Work
Lena Dominelli

Working with Abused Children
Celia Doyle

Evaluating for Good Practice
Angela Everitt and Pauline Hardiker

Applied Research for Better Practice
Angela Everitt, Pauline Hardiker,
Jane Littlewood and
Audrey Mullender

Student Supervision in Social Work
Kathy Ford and Alan Jones

Working with Rural Communities
David Francis and Paul Henderson

Children, their Families and the Law
Michael D. A. Freeman

Family Work with Elderly People
Alison Froggatt

Child Sexual Abuse
Danya Glaser and Stephen Frosh

Computers in Social Work
Bryan Glastonbury

Working with Families
Gill Gorell Barnes

Women, Management and Care
Cordelia Grimwood and Ruth Popplestone

Women and Social Work
Jalna Hanmer and Daphne Statham

Youth Work
Tony Jeffs and Mark Smith (eds)

Problems of Childhood and Adolescence
Michael Kerfoot and Alan Butler

Communication in Social Work
Joyce Lishman

Working with Violence
Carol Lupton and Terry Gillespie (eds)

Social Work with Older People
Mary Marshall and Mary Dixon

Applied Psychology for Social Workers
Paula Nicolson and Rowan Bayne

Crisis Intervention in Social Services
Kieran O'Hagan

Social Work with Disabled People
Michael Oliver

Care Management
Joan Orme and Bryan Glastonbury

Social Care in the Community
Malcolm Payne

Working in Teams
Malcolm Payne

Working with Young Offenders
John Pitts

Effective Groupwork
Michael Preston-Shoot

Effective Probation Practice
Peter Raynor, David Smith and Maurice
Vanstone

Social Work with the Dying and Bereaved
Carole R. Smith

Child Care and the Courts
Carole R. Smith, Mary T. Lane and
Terry Walsh

Criminology for Social Work
David Smith

Social Work and Housing
Gill Stewart and John Stewart

Focus on Families
Christine Stones

Anti-Discriminatory Practice
Neil Thompson

Dealing with Stress
Neil Thompson, Michael Murphy and Steve
Stradling

Working with Mental illness
Derek Tilbury

Community Work
Alan Twelvetrees

Working with Offenders
Hilary Walker and Bill Beaumont (eds)

Social Work with Older People

Third Edition

Mary Marshall

and

Mary Dixon

MACMILLAN

First edition (*Social Work with Old People*) 1983
Reprinted 1985
Second edition 1990
Reprinted 1990, 1993
Third edition (*Social Work with Older People*) 1996

Published by
MACMILLAN PRESS LTD
Houndmills, Basingstoke, Hampshire RG21 6XS
and London
Companies and representatives
throughout the world

ISBN 0-333-64168-X

A catalogue record for this book is available
from the British Library.

10   9   8   7   6   5   4   3   2   1
04 03 02 01 00 99 98 97 96 95

Printed in Malaysia

Series Standing Order (Practical Social Work)

If you would like to receive future titles in this series as they
are published, you can make use of our standing order facility.
To take a standing order please contact your bookseller or, in
case of difficulty, write to us at the address below with your name
and address and the name of the series. Please state with which
title you wish to begin your standing order. (If you live outside
the UK we may not have the rights for your area, in which case
we will forward your order to the publisher concerned.)

Standing Order Service, Macmillan Distribution Ltd,
Houndmills, Basingstoke, Hampshire, RG21 2XS, England

Contents

Preface to the Third Edition   vii

1 What to Expect from this Book   1

2 Knowing Your Population   7
   Older people's lives   9
   Men and women   12
   Poverty   14
   What is old?   15
   Location   16
   Housing   17
   Health   18
   Using facts and figures   21

3 Older People – Expectations and Experiences   23
   Retirement   23
   Feeling old   26
   Ageism   28
   A positive view   32
   Older people as volunteers   34
   Older people as carers   36

4 Getting Started – Issues in Social Work   40
   The hospital setting   41
   The area team setting   46
   Rural locations   50
   Starting and stopping contact   52
   Using information   57
   Records and language   59
   Supervision   62
   A bottom line   64
   Social work practice and methods   67
   Self-care   74
   Knowledge   77

5 The Assessment Process   **86**
    The Referral   88
    Making contact   90
    The first visit   92
    Observation and assessment   95
    Risk   104
    Charges   106
    Putting together the care package   108
    Records   113
    Reviews   114
    Quality   114
    Particular areas of work   116
    Moving into longstay care   116
    Abuse   122
    Death and loss   123
    Discharge from hospital   126

6 Working with Others   **128**
    The social services team   129
    The health team   130
    The voluntary and private sector   135
    Important others   137
    The last word   138

Appendix   139
    I   *Arthritis*   139
   II   *Dementia*   140
  III   *Heart Problems*   142
   IV   *Strokes*   143

References   145

Index   148

Preface to the Third Edition

Mary Dixon wrote most of this book because she is a social worker still in day to day contact with older people; Mary Marshall works almost exclusively with staff. It is a joint book for two reasons. The first is that we have learnt a lot of what we know together. We are both social workers who have a preference for working with older people and who have mainly worked in this field. We have talked for years together about our work and the books we found useful. We have both had ill, older relatives who have taught us a great deal. Although Mary Marshall wrote the first two editions, Mary Dixon was a powerful influence and commented on the text as it was written. The roles have been reversed in this book. It was decided to put both names on it since the text is based on the first two editions although the updating has been very substantial. Very many thanks from both of us to the friends, colleagues, relatives and older people and their families who have contributed to our thinking and experience.

A special word of thanks to Joe McElholm and John Bishop for their very helpful reading, comments and contributions to the text.

MARY MARSHALL
MARY DIXON

1

What to Expect from this Book

This book is addressed at all those wishing to work with old people. It is written with the belief that social work has a great deal to offer and that, for too long, the skills and expertise that social workers can bring have been denied to some of the most vulnerable people in our communities.

As social workers begin their careers it is likely that they will develop some expertise and interest in working with particular care or user groups. Amongst the majority of area team social workers, work with children and families has long been regarded as the most vital and interesting. In working with young people and young families, social workers seem to see the clear potential to assist individuals to change their lives for the better. By contrast social work with old people has been seen as having limited scope and challenge and as being bound up with the arranging of practical services for those needing help.

With all the demands made on social work time, a constant rationing and prioritisation of resources has to take place. The legislative requirements of work with young people and the priority this demands, has often meant that social work teams have been hard pressed to achieve the fine balancing act necessary to meet the needs of other care groups. In this situation, work with old people has often lost out for a second time or been delegated to less experienced, unqualified or trainee workers. In many departments this has had the effect of perpetuating the view that work with old people is not a priority for social workers or their managers. It is, rather, seen as low status work involving only straightforward and simple tasks.

We intend in this book to put work with old people clearly on the map. Social work is a vitally important service for old people. Social work with old people means at minimum, developing excellent assessment skills and being prepared to work with complex family relationships. There are numerous other skills to be learned and used. As a result it is both rewarding and challenging. It calls for inventive and imaginative problem solvers and as a consequence demands brave workers who are able to fight on behalf of the older person.

Within the last few years the NHS and Community Care Act 1990 has placed centre stage, the need for social services departments to develop their social work services to adults. This new legislation has meant a turnaround in the way services are organised. In nearly all departments old people come in contact with social workers having been referred for an assessment. Most departments now have a range of community care groupings to serve, of which old people form by far the largest. For this reason, if no other, social workers must now begin to develop the skills needed to work alongside older people and their carers. Many who are coming new to working with old people will be wondering about the skills and knowledge they are expected to have. Our hope for this new third edition is that it will provide a starting point for workers to feel confident in this area of work and will offer a sound skill and knowledge base with which to begin.

The introduction of community care legislation has meant enormous change for social workers. Tasks and responsibilities have changed and departments have been reshaped and restructured to meet the new demands placed upon them. The legislation driving this change, has been very much a response to the shift in emphasis in society's view about the individual's and the wider community's responsibility to care for and help itself. The Conservative government that came to power in 1979 had as a key component to its manifesto a strong ethos on family responsibility and self-reliance. Such a view holds the family and the community as the appropriate first avenues to provide help to those in need. The legislation reflects this view. Social workers have traditionally had a major role in working alongside relatives, neighbours and friends to encourage and maintain the vital community support that these networks offer.

This will continue to be a key task for social workers, particularly as local authorities increase their emphasis on the development of respite and home support services to assist those who provide this care.

As many social workers will know, this, however, is only half the picture. Social workers often find themselves working in situations where reliance on family and community support is not an option. It may be that help from outside an individual's immediate community is the only source of help available. In some situations it may also be the most desirable. Many older people simply do not have available relatives or a supportive local community. Those who are very old may have outlived their families and friends. Others who have been institutionalised for a long period may have lost touch with families and neighbours. Others may have been abused by their relatives. Old people without suitable support are very likely to be solely reliant on the formal care services accessed via community care assessments. The NHS and Community Care Act 1990 has given to local authority social services departments a very clear role to assist individuals to secure the help they need. The Act has placed formal responsibilities on departments to assess and set in place packages of care and to monitor the delivery of such care arrangements. The undertaking of community care assessments in order to produce individual care plans has now become the major social work function carried out with older people. The demand for assessments as the key to services has in turn affected the organisation of social work services within departments. Local authorities have, in the last couple of years, tended towards locating social workers in specialist care teams rather than in generic social work teams. The introduction of this new legislation has also led, in some areas, to a new flexibility as to who undertakes this assessment work. Many local authorities now have care managers who are not social workers. Others have sought to establish mixed expertise teams to undertake the required assessments. This has meant home help organisers (HHO) and occupational therapists (OT) joining teams and being involved in tasks previously seen as the preserve of social workers. In some local authorities multi agency teams are in operation, with district nurses and health visitors working alongside social workers in the new community care assessment teams. This mix of skills and divergence of expertise has a great deal to offer both to social workers and older people alike.

As well as changing the way social work is organised, the practical resources provided by departments are also under review. The government is requiring multi agency provision. Local authorities are no longer required to maintain a full range of day care, domiciliary and residential care services for all community care groups. Changes in legislation and guidelines from government, are now encouraging social services departments to explore what assistance may be offered by service providers other than those within the statutory sector. The notion of services being tendered for amongst a variety of other providers has been common practice in the NHS for the last five years. The policies developed to support these ideas are now fast becoming an intrinsic part of the framework within which social services departments now operate. Such developments have encouraged a proliferation in the number of privately run residential and domestic support services available to older people who require care. Voluntary sector organisations are, likewise, developing an increasingly important role in providing direct care services. In some instances they are the main providers of home support and day care services particularly in some of the more rural areas of Britain.

Working with this new mixed economy of service providers and the onset of charges are changes we have to make the most of. The growth and variety amongst service providers that workers can now expect to access, should encourage us to insist on a flexibility amongst providers and so be truly needs led. With this flexibility there must also follow opportunities for us to encourage and assist individuals to exercise some choice in the services they receive. Social workers are increasingly acting as assessors-cum-brokers when putting together packages of care. What must not be lost, however, is the chance to see ourselves as a resource for the older person. We too offer a service; by using skills to help people face what might be painful adjustments and losses in their lives.

When focusing on the assessment process, we need to be able to understand and take on board other areas of need including those of carers. In order to achieve appropriate assessments, we should strive to develop a knowledge and understanding about the health problems older people can experience. It is not enough to know that someone has arthritis without having some concept of what this might mean in terms of living with stiffness, constant pain and the frustration of having to depend on others. The changing demands dictated by needs led assessments call on us to have a flexible approach to our area of work and to be prepared to step into areas of expertise not previously ours. This may mean, for example, having some idea about how to measure the correct height for a walking stick. We may struggle to assess a person's mobility if we are unable to judge whether the stick the person is using is the right height for them. We need now to prepare ourselves for this more all round approach. We hope this new edition will act as a pointer for much of this knowledge. Where those new to this work do not have specialist knowledge or where additional knowledge is required, then they should not be afraid to ask others for help. Asking for help should not be an onerous task. Other colleagues are usually very willing to share what they know and indeed it can cement a working relationship.

Although this book is primarily directed at social workers it could also be useful to staff undertaking work with older people in numerous different settings. There is inevitably a degree of overlap in the skills we all need to work with older people. We hope this book is useful to staff such as home helps, OTs, community nurses and staff in any longstay setting.

The areas we intend to cover in this book will relate to what we feel to be good social work practice. Individuals who may be new to social work or who are embarking on training, possibly through the Diploma in Social Work (DIPSW) or National and Scottish Vocational Qualifications (NVQ/SVQ) may find some helpful material in the following chapters. We hope that readers will find this book accessible and to be of use at whatever level they work. The establishment of specialist community care teams has meant that many staff who have formally worked exclusively in other fields such as child care, are now coming new to working with older people. In such a situation workers may feel bewildered and de-skilled by these new demands. This book is also written for them.

In order to make social work distinct when reference is made to the range of statutory services we will talk in terms of social services departments. We do this in full realisation that this is English usage and will not read comfortably for people working in Scotland and Northern Ireland. It did however seem to us to be very cumbersome to mention the three different terms whenever we referred to the employing department.

A final point on style. Everybody referred to in this book whose sex is not clear is assumed to be female. This is different from the usual custom, but the reality is that the great majority of social workers and older people are women. The reason for this decision is to avoid the clumsiness of compromises like him/her or s/he. For similar reasons throughout the text we will make reference to line managers rather than team leaders or seniors and will talk about individuals and people rather than users or service users. The term black, in accordance with the Commission for Racial Equality definition, will be used throughout, unless a specific point related to a specific racial group is being illustrated.

2

Knowing Your Population

Few can have failed to recognise that there are now growing numbers of old people in our communities. This is an issue of concern and interest for all local authority social services departments, who must plan for and develop services to meet the needs of their local populations. The production of such plans generates a great deal of information that can be of use to social work teams. This information can assist in the process of seeing the make up of the local older population in terms of, for example, concentrations of very old people or types of housing which might be difficult for older people.

There are various explanations for the increasing numbers of old people in the population. A partial answer is that we are living longer. The last 100 years have seen massive changes as to how people live. General improvements to housing stock, sanitation arrangements, cleaner water, inoculation against diseases and better food supplies have all assisted our standard of living to improve. This has meant that more people have survived infancy and lived into adulthood. In the last 150 years the infant mortality rate has decreased from 148 per 1000 births to 9 per 1000 (England and Wales). It is estimated that in the relatively short period of the last 70 years the average life expectancy in the UK has increased from 63 years to 74 years.

The most recent population figures available for the UK are provided by the Office of Population Censuses and Surveys (OPCS) and include population projections for 1985 to 2025. These figures inform us that in 1991 five million people were aged between 65 and 74, 3.1 million were aged 75 to 84 and 0.9 million aged 85 and over. This gives a total of nine million people over retirement age. If you include those over 60 this takes the figure up to just under ten million. From a total UK population figure of 55 million it can therefore be estimated that just over one in five of the population are over retirement age. A slight decline in the numbers of those aged 65 to 74 will occur by the turn of the century, but the numbers over 75 will rise steadily for the next 30 years, peaking at 3.9 million aged 75 to 84 and 1.3 million aged 85 plus, by the year 2025. Roughly two thirds of this total number are likely to be women. The 1994 edition of *Social Trends* (Central Statistical Office) suggests different figures for the older population. These figures provide total for the 65+ mid year projections as 2001 – 15.6 million, 2011 – 16.6 million, 2021 – 19.2 million. Given the variations that can take place between projections, affected as they are by population growth and mortality rates, close examinations of local figures are essential.

These figures clearly highlight that old age covers a wide age span. The numbers living into their nineties possibly their hundreds, suggest that many people who retire at 65 face a potential 30 years ahead as pensioners. Such an age range encompasses at least two if not three generations of experience and difference. Those in the younger age range of 65 to 74 will have a different view of welfare services and, as a result may have different expectations of social services. The older age group, 75 plus, may view welfare services as charity and hold a firmer belief in self reliance and independence. The experiences of those aged 90 will be different from those aged 75 and different again from those aged between 65 and 70. Older people are clearly not one large homogenous group. They have very different experiences, wants and needs. The attitudes of an individual will often reflect the events through which they have lived. It is therefore important for us to take on board the traditions and times that have helped to shape people's childhood and adult experiences. In doing this, we can begin to empathise with the complexity of people's lives and to communicate and offer help in a manner that is acceptable and appropriate.

Older people's lives

A useful starting point is to consider some of the events that individuals will have faced, particularly in their early years. Those born in Britain at around the turn of the century were in their teens and twenties during the First World War. They lost their brothers and fathers on the battlefields of France. The First World War took from the population thousands of young men, leaving behind countless widows and young women. These women faced a future without men, they would never find husbands and would have to live without the comfort of children. Fewer men in the population directly affected the birth rate, which remained low for over 20 years from the end of the First World War. Of those who did survive, many went on to rear families who then gave their lives in the Second World War.

Mrs Holden lost her first husband in France in 1918. She raised three sons who then joined the navy to fight in the Second World War. Two were lost with the sinking of HMS Edinburgh, one returned disabled and so scared by his experiences that he never left the house again. Her second husband whom she married in 1938 died when Liverpool docks were bombed. Her disabled son took his own life after she had cared for him for nearly 20 years. Mrs Holden tried to make sense of her life by talking incessantly about her sons. She rang social workers daily saying that she needed help. She needed very little practical help but wanted, rather, to talk constantly about her losses. We cannot really know what such terrible loss meant to her. However, workers can and should understand her need and that of others like her to talk and have someone listen. Sometimes all that can be done is to listen and we should always be prepared to give time for this. Giving ourselves as a resource to soak up some of the pain can be as important as providing any amount of practical help.

Those who are now in their 60s and 70s can carry the experience of equally hard times. These might be their own experiences or those of their parents. Mrs Gain, for example, a widow aged 71 has a regular party piece – to tell of the time she saw her first banana at the age of 18. She tried to eat it not knowing that it had to be peeled first. Her telling of this tale reflects tough times living with rationing and other shortages which her family experienced even though the immediate threat of war was over.

Those who were born in another land may have had to face leaving their home, knowing that they would probably never see their grandparents or parents again. Facing the pressures of life alone, learning new ways, a new language and possibly experiencing discrimination, may have felt like a constant struggle. All of these experiences will inform the way an individual might cope with difficulties and relate to those trying to help them.

Understanding the ups and downs of the birthrate and other population trends can help our understanding of some of the background issues we uncover when we are arranging the care and support an individual may need. For some people living longer means being disabled for many years and possibly needing assistance to maintain independence. Family are usually the first line of support to provide such assistance. However, with a low birth rate, extended family networks are not always readily available. In addition families were depleted by war and a sizeable number of people have sought to make other countries their home. This was true of many people born prior to the Second World War. Many saw the opportunity for a better life in places like Australia and New Zealand, than could be offered by a war scarred and ration bound Britain. Emigration played a major role in distancing family and affecting support networks. Between 1946 and 1959 nearly a million people left Britain to make homes on the other side of the world. In parts of Liverpool, large numbers of older people can tell of a son or daughter in Canada, this being the destination of many of the passenger ships passing through Liverpool in the late 1940s and early 1950s.

At the same time as hundreds of thousands left the UK, others came to make Britain their home. These people now figure importantly in our ageing population. If social services departments wish to develop services for older people, it is critical that they acknowledge the full racial and cultural mix that exists in today's Britain. This means ensuring that services are relevant and sensitive to the needs of those from different backgrounds and cultures. For over a hundred years many Irish men and women have been coming to live and work in Britain's big cities. London, Birmingham and Glasgow all have thriving

Irish communities. Jewish people, originating from across Europe, have since the 1900s established communities in most of the large population centres. In the late 50s and 60s young men and women came from the Caribbean to work in the growing transport and public service industries. Many countries on the African coast have had a long history of providing seafarers to work the big supply ships that travelled the world. These men from Sierra Leone, Ethiopia and Somalia travelled and settled in the ports of Britain and raised families here. For these men who came in the 1900s it is their children who are part of the ageing population. Some may have an identity that is geordie and scouse as well as black and African. Not all, however, made the choice to come here. Some had to leave their homelands because of persecution or as refugees; others have experienced accidents of fate. Mr Ali whose home was in Somalia had worked at sea his entire life, including a period in the Second World War as a sailor in the Merchant Navy. His ship docked in Liverpool on his 65th birthday and so he had to get off, leaving his wife and six children some 3000 miles away. It was only when he became ill and was admitted to hospital that his plight became known. He had been unhappily stuck in the UK for eight years before a social worker was able to arrange for him to return to his family.

Many of those who have settled in the UK are now beginning to grow old here. Some communities of longer standing have developed their own welfare services. Jewish welfare societies provide meals services, residential care and a host of other social work services to their communities in many parts of Britain including important therapy services for those traumatised by their experiences at the hands of the Nazis. Younger communities including those from Africa and Asia are now also developing similar services to offer contact and combat isolation. Many of these communities now have significant numbers of older members. For example, out of a 17.4 per cent total ethnic minority population (that originated from the new Commonwealth) in England and Wales approximately 4 per cent are over 60/65. Little research exists that can help us pinpoint the age mix of this population, for example, whether people are in their 60s and 70s or in their 80s. However, it is possible to imagine that unless people emigrated to Britain when in their middle years, then the 4 per cent are likely to be made up of the young old: aged 65 to 74. This 4 per cent can be further broken down via the origins given on census records. This divides the 4 per cent as: 2 per cent West Indies, 1 per cent Indian sub continent and 1 per cent Pakistan. Although these figures are useful indicators, they are not able to provide a picture of the ageing black population who have Britain as their country of origin. There are also shortfalls in information when looking at ageing populations from other parts of the world such as China, Africa, Poland, the Ukraine and the Mediterranean countries. This is an issue which warrants much closer examination and research.

Those who have an identity which is British born black will often have different experiences and needs from those from ethnic minority populations who were born elsewhere. One experience however, which will be held in common, will be the double edged sword of ageism and racism. An individual's experiences of living in a predominately western, white, protestant society will clearly affect their expectations and use of welfare services.

Men and women

Another area of interest in our ageing population is the balance that exists between the numbers of men and women. The effects on society of wars and other hardships, and the fact that men traditionally die younger than women, have tended to skew our ageing population so that there are now a lot more older women than men. In the age group 60 to 74 there are 127 women to every 100 men. This uneven balance grows to 200 women to every 100 men over 75 and then on to 327 women to every 100 men for those over 80. For many women who have been used to a life full of men it must seem very odd to no longer have them around. For some very old women, men may have had a central role in their lives as the family decision makers. Women in this position, who have always been in the role of adopting the choices made by the fathers, brothers and husbands are likely to need assistance to practise their own decision making skills. As social workers, faced with making decisions every day, it requires a great deal of patience and tact to work with individuals who find this a difficult task.

Mrs Wild caused her social worker much exasperation in this regard. She was unsure about whether to accept a home help into her home. She could only focus on the fact that her now dead husband would not have strangers in his house, even though the struggle to care for him on her own had seriously jeopardized her health. His feelings and decisions about not having help hung heavily over Mrs Wild making it very difficult for her to see her own need for assistance. We social workers must appreciate that, for some, decisions are not easy. Furthermore the decisions we are often keen for people to make are in themselves fairly monumental. To make a major decision, for example, to leave one's own home either temporarily or permanently, requires a great deal of thinking and talking about. We need to be mindful of these possible difficulties and be sensitive to what might be our own impatience to push people towards a decision before they are ready.

With women making up two thirds of the old population, old age is clearly the women's issue for the next decade. Women will be the majority of those making use of social services. This may mean raising questions about equal opportunity of access to help. Meg Bond in her paper 'Women's Work in a Woman's World' (1979), about the home help service, highlights how men are more likely to be seen as in need of practical help within the home. This was not an issue about disability but more that men are less likely to know how to perform housework tasks and so need assistance which would not be offered to women with the same lack of knowledge. Men are likely to have these tasks performed for them by home helps. The development of quality assurance measures should assist social services departments to make sure that these issues are on their agendas. Those with an interest in equality issues and women's experience of ageist discrimination will find *Look Me in the Eye* by Macdonald and Rich (1983) and *Over the Hill* by Baba Cooper (1988) particularly interesting reading.

The vast majority of older women whom social workers meet will be living alone. 10.1 per cent of women are likely to have been single throughout their lives and, depending on the age range, between 21 and 52 per cent will be widowed or divorced and now alone. Living alone may be by choice for some, for others it is the situation they find themselves in after the loss of a partner. As a new experience it can provoke anxiety and fear. Once on her own, Mrs Ward found it very difficult to let her son leave after each of his daily visits. Her fear of being alone meant that she spent the night listening out for every sound. The introduction of a neighbour who lived in the same block of flats, to befriend Mrs Ward, provided her with re-assurance that even though she was on her own, she could find help just along the landing.

Some women may find living alone very isolating. For those who have been traditionally based in the home, there may have been little chance to develop a wide network of friendships once family have moved away. All of this can lead to quite powerful feelings of isolation, as individuals recognise that they have little or no emotional support to call upon. Many social workers will have felt at one time or another that what an older person has really needed, has been a friend to talk to and confide in, not a social worker calling.

For those who have lived on their own for a number of years, or who have not created their own families, friends are likely to be a major source of support. We tend to develop the bulk of our friendships amongst those we study with and work beside. Social workers need always to acknowledge the importance of friendships in people's lives. For those on their own, they are the emotional equivalent of having family or partner support. Friends may be involved with old people as carers or as advocates. We should always make room for their views to be heard.

Poverty

In listening to older women talk about their lives, money and their worry about the lack of it is a key influence on whether people feel they have a good quality of life. Many women now in old age may not have had long periods of employment in their younger lives. They will have had time at home to raise families, some having given up work as soon as they married. In pension terms this means that many women are reliant on their partners' contributions (or lack of them) to secure their level of benefit.

Poverty of course is not just an issue for women. Men who have worked for years in low paid manual jobs are unlikely to have been in a position to save towards supplementing their retirement pensions. Increasing numbers of people are now living for 20 to 30 years on a retirement pension. Many scrape by on a pension that might provide enough for them to eat and keep themselves warm from week to week. However the replacement of clothes, household goods and repairs to a home are impossible to save for on such a fixed weekly income. Some of the younger old people aged 65 to 74 may have had more opportunity to pay in to a work related pension and so have additional money to see them through retirement. Since the later 1980s there have been added incentives from government for people to think about providing for their own futures through private pension plans. The traditional reliance on national insurance and the old age pension is changing.

What is old?

In looking at who are the older population, it is important that we pause and recognise how easy it has been to slip into an acceptance of 60 and 65 as a legitimate definition of old. For those of us heading towards our forties and fifties, 60 or 65 seems ridiculously close as the time when we will be regarded as old and cease to do paid work. 60 or 65 heralds retirement from work for the majority of people in Britain, but not for all. Some people will choose to continue to work beyond retirement age, most commonly on a part-time rather than full-time basis. Census information indicates that 7 per cent of women and 17 per cent of men aged between 65 and 69 are continuing to work past retirement. Following the budget of November 1994 the government of the day have given notice that they intend to increase the retirement age for both men and women to 65. This decision may mean that companies retain their most experienced workers and develop fewer opportunities for younger people to join the workforce.

In Britain, there are opposing views about the age at which someone should cease to work. Some people are counting the days to retirement, others are keen to continue to work. For example, 73 year old Mrs Hamid is active in her son's newsagent business. She works, as she has always done, to play her part in the family business. She would only cease to work if physical problems impeded her from continuing. Cultural views of what constitutes old age also vary significantly. In some middle eastern cultures it is becoming a grandparent which marks passing into elder status.

For some, retirement can come earlier than 65. The remodelling of workforces and the decline in some industries has meant that increasing numbers are taking early retirement from work. For some this is a choice; for others, a result of redundancy. Some companies and industries offer support to workers in this, by running pre-retirement courses and counselling services to help individuals adjust to this new phase in their lives. The concept of early retirement has led to the development of a growing number of service industries targeting insurance, holidays and leisure activities at the 'new old': the 50 plus age group. It will be interesting to see if, in times ahead, retirement and old age begin to be seen as separate episodes in people's lives. Retirement might well become the period between 55 and 65, before people are deemed officially old.

Location

As with age range and gender there are issues for social workers linked to where people live. The location of individuals has an impact on their lives. Informal networks and provision of services are geographically tied. Where you live may well affect what help you can access. It is not uncommon to hear people talk about Costa Geriatica, referring to the significant numbers of older people who have moved to coastal communities for their retirement years. Retiring to the seaside may have its attractions. However the development of poor health, the loss of a partner and dependence on help from others, can mean that services run the risk of being over stretched.

Coastal resorts are not the only places with higher than average proportions of older people in the general population. Many city centres are also experiencing a large proportion of older people. For the most part this has been the result of younger families moving to outer city housing estates, often to escape cramped housing and to seek jobs sited on outlying industrial estates. Mrs Jones, who had lived in the middle of town and raised her family of five in a tiny two up two down house, was solely reliant on her daughter Jane. Jane and her husband lived 12 miles away in an outer city housing estate. The journey into town to see her mother involved getting three buses, hours spent travelling and a great deal of expense. The resulting infrequent contact was of deep regret to both of them.

Demographic changes within the population are also occurring in a great many rural areas, where they now have high proportions of older people. This has implications for the development of services. The situation in mid-Wales for example, highlights a picture common to other rural communities. The mid-1985 estimates of population had the over 65s as the following percentages of the population: Gwynedd 21.7 per cent and Powys 20.7 per cent. These percentages are set to rise until the turn of the century. With between one in four and one in five of some rural populations likely to be pensioners, flexible thinking will need to take place to make sure that services are available to all who need them. In some areas it may be voluntary and community organisations which are best placed to run services and provide the necessary support. In smaller communities people tend to have more regular day to day contact with one another. The community is likely to be the social focus for those who live within it. With contacts already established informal networks can be more readily available to help those in need. This is not, of course, always the case since some individuals require a lot more help than their similarly elderly neighbours can provide. Some individuals, for a variety of reasons, may not elicit a helping response. Workers may therefore be called upon to use skills to support individuals and to mediate their needs with other community members.

Housing

In knowing where older people are, we also need to consider the types of accommodation in which they might live. Only 4 per cent of the older population live in institutional care. This is a very small percentage of all those over 65, but for social workers these may be the bulk of individuals with whom we have contact. Old people are more likely to live in older accommodation. Older housing stock is more likely to be without, what have come to be regarded, as basic amenities. Of the half a million homes which lack the necessities of hot water, an inside toilet and a bath, 55 per cent are occupied by pensioners. Older houses are also likely to be more difficult to heat and may possibly be in need of some repair. All of this can mean a number of hidden costs, which some individuals will struggle to meet. It is not uncommon to find people restricting their use of a house to one or two rooms in order to save on fuel and other costs. Housing can become unsuitable in numerous ways: stairs in tenements, poor repair and insulation, no downstairs toilet and so on. We are only slowly learning how to knit housing into community care. This can be a real struggle with its many complicated organisational and financial issues.

Health

Those living into old age have then a number of major issues to contend with. They may live alone, have little family support to call upon and have to survive in poorly maintained houses or flats. Individuals may also be living in a culture which is not their own and which does not appear to offer them a great deal. Furthermore, there is the potential for difficulties due to poor health. Those over the age of 74 are more likely to experience health problems than the rest of the general population. Health problems at this age will usually directly affect an individual's daily life. Often such difficulties are to do with mobility, sensory impairment or chronic pain. Social workers do not have a good track record in taking account of these factors, so this book makes a special point of covering them. You will find sections on the major health problems in the appendices.

Health problems affect large numbers of people over 74. For example hearing loss is a problem for 45 per cent of those aged over 80. 70 per cent of people aged over 65 are likely to have discomfort and difficulty in movement due to arthritis or rheumatism. 25 per cent of the older population have a degree of poor vision that requires corrective surgery. Living with such disabling conditions requires some adjustment to daily routine and activity. Coming to terms with a new way of life caused by any of these problems takes determination and often calls for inventive adaptation. Living with chronic ill-health, particularly over a long period, can be very debilitating. An individual's daily routine may have to be planned around managing what they can do, when they are able to do it, given pain and other discomforts.

Mental ill-health is also a feature of old age for a significant number of people. It is estimated that about one in ten people aged 65 and over have some degree of dementia. In the 80 plus group this rises to something like one in four. Other mental health problems also feature in old age. Depression is as common as dementia but is largely hidden. Some people get paraphrenia which is the schizophrenia of old age. Both depression and paraphrenia can respond to drug treatment. Dementia is the mental illness social workers see most of. Working with people who have dementia is challenging work. Families too will need ongoing support to help them live through the effects of this illness and to achieve some acceptance of the changes that will come to affect the person for whom they care. We need to develop skills including a flexibility of approach and an ability to work very closely with the range of other service providers who will also have a role in dementia care.

The degree and complexity of health problems which older people can experience does not, unfortunately, always match up to their use of health services. The first point of contact for most people will be their GP, which may be because they have sought help and may be as a result of an assessment visit, which GPs are required to offer. This is not always a successful contact. GPs are seen as busy, important people and for some older people are too important to trouble unless symptoms are specific and serious. A successful Well Older Persons clinic in Barnet provided a solution to this difficulty. Monthly sessions enabled older people to call in and discuss the odd aches and pains they experienced, with which they would not have wanted to bother the doctor. Such a service provides a useful early screening for potential problems as well as reassurance to those with minor difficulties. Those who are now in their 70s and 80s will have lived through a time when free health care was not available. Indeed those aged over 60 may well be able to call to mind stories about parents or grandparents not seeking medical treatment because it had to be paid for. Not having the doctor as the first port of call may have aided the development of some interesting and effective methods of self treatment. It is also equally likely to have helped reinforce the view that the doctor is only to be fetched when there is real evidence of a serious problem. We need to understand why an individual might have anxiety about summoning a doctor. It could be the fear of being a trouble, or of hearing something they already suspect, being confirmed.

Being able to switch GPs easily, if you are not happy with the service, has only been seen as a real possibility in recent times. Previously if someone was not happy with the service, the answer was often to avoid calling the doctor. We need to encourage older people to think of all of their options in situations such as these. If a GP is not providing the service they need, it is important to suggest that they can shop around and find somebody else to provide their medical care. We need to know how to set a change of GP in motion.

Significant numbers of old people are likely to have what we have now come to regard as health threatening habits. These are principally smoking and drinking which may impact on a person's health in a number of ways. We need to understand that it is always worth aiming for a healthy lifestyle. Taking the view that they might as well be unhealthy because they are nearing the end of their lives is an unhelpful approach, and flies in the face of evidence that even very old people can be more comfortable and healthier if they stop smoking or eat nourishing food.

One of the problems is that many older people accept a degree of disability and illness as part of growing older. They complain of feeling ill and old only when they are feeling down or depressed. Feeling good makes more difference to people's lives than just how mobile they might be or whether breathlessness is a problem. Indeed older people often report that their health is fine even when they are quite severely disabled. This may mean, as we have said before, that they fail to seek help with physical problems which they see as something to be endured. Conversely hypochondriasis is a sign of depression in older people. Depressed people can be very preoccupied with their symptoms even when they are, relatively speaking, in good health.

Using facts and figures

It is always worthwhile spending time to find out about the local population. Most social services departments will have a research and development section. Such a section may be based at headquarters or out at divisional or district level. In our experience staff in these sections are always pleased to be asked for information about a local population. There may also be statistical sources within the office. Social services departments hold registers and listings which can be very useful. The disabled register or the aids and adaptation waiting lists can be used to identify caring situations and so target information about carers groups and respite services. One area team sent a 'do it yourself' benefit checksheet to all on the office occupational therapy waiting lists. This brought 22 visits to the office for help to complete Attendance Allowance claims. It created some work, but it also made those on the list feel as if they were being offered some support and were not just forgotten. It also brought at least half this number additional income. Some of this may feel like creating new work, but will help carers and older people to make choices for themselves and to come along to offices better informed to discuss needs for services.

If you find that your area has a sizeable older population, it may be important to undertake some kind of information drive to make people aware of what social services can offer. A particular campaign on, say, respite care could be targeted at blocks of flats or sheltered housing schemes where there are obvious populations who might have an interest in this service. Knowing the numbers of old people in the area will help the social work team see if referral numbers match with the population figures. If they do not, issues might need to be addressed about why older people are not contacting the social services department. If older people are not approaching the area team for help, is it because they do not want help or is it because they do not know where the office is and that it can offer a source of assistance? The team can address this in a number of ways. Providing an information stall in a shopping centre or using events such as Dementia Awareness Week are ideal ways of informing the public about what is on offer.

In summary, population figures and demographic profiles can help to plan services and anticipate the likely demands for help from a community. They also assist in the process of thinking about the distinctions that exist within the older population and helps towards an understanding of the lives that old people lead and have led. As a general rule of thumb, it is possible to say that those over the age of 75 will have a greater chance of being female, alone, poor, badly housed and in poor health.

3

Older People – Expectations and Experiences

By the time people reach the age of 65, 88 per cent are retired. Retirement and the release of time it brings can mean a new lease of life. Freedom from work may mean time to develop existing interests or to find new challenges. It can also mean, for some, facing a future where ill health and poverty have an increasing effect on the quality of their lives. In this chapter we want to reflect on some issues which have a major bearing on the lives of older people such as the impact of retirement and the negative impact of ageism. We want also to focus on the many positive contributions that older people make. Older people are active as volunteers and carers and as such are a rich source of support with whom we can work.

Retirement

Retirement, whatever it brings, is the gateway to a long and significant period of people's lives. Those who retire at 65 may face a possible 30 years ahead. Living through these years will mean facing change and making adjustments. How people deal with change will reflect their circumstances, life experiences and the support networks they have around to sustain them. The potential volume of changes to be experienced will increase as people get older.

In looking, in Chapter 2, at the numbers of older people in

the general population, it has been helpful to think in terms of at least two different populations: the 'young old' (65–74) and the 'old' (75+). This is a useful way to continue. These two groupings may have very different ways of dealing with change. The young old and the old will have different pressures and problems to face. They may also have very different expectations of what their retirement years will bring. The attitudes that people carry with them into retirement will have the strongest impact on how they go on to develop this period of their lives. It can be a very active busy time or it can be God's waiting room. A positive attitude and the desire to keep finding enjoyment wherever possible is often the key to a successful old age.

Of the many changes and adjustments to be faced, the first and the most significant is retirement itself. Retirement is one of the most important milestones in western industrial societies. Its significance is overwhelming for all who have been reared to see their usefulness in terms of occupation. Work provides social interaction and for those who have retired this is often what they miss the most. It also provides the scaffolding for people's lives, it denotes their place in society, how others see them and how they expect to be treated. Some people may experience retirement as a loss and, as with any loss, it must be made sense of before the person can move on. Retirement or, as Phillipson in his book, *Capitalism and the Construction of Old Age* (1982) more correctly suggests, enforced retirement, dictates that those reaching 60 and 65 (or even 50 these days) are seen as non active producers and in need of physical, financial and psychological support. The task that Phillipson sees for social work, is not to collude with the low expectations that many older people have about how they will be treated and about the value they credit themselves as having.

It seems likely that people who prepare for retirement cope better with it. But most pre-retirement education and preparation is given too little and too late. Given that money and health are the main indicators of life satisfaction in retirement, planning for retirement should take place much earlier than it does. Mid-life planning courses have begun to emerge in the last ten years. But for the most part those receiving pre-retirement education are receiving this only a week or two before retirement is due, leaving little time for real thinking about the future to take place.

Added to whatever mental adjustments are necessary, retirement can also be a big shock to the system. An individual's body clock may continue to wake them at seven o'clock in the morning in order to get ready for work. Meal timing and what is eaten may be affected by the change in daily routine. If the physical demands of work have stopped then aches, pain and stiffness that were previously kept at bay may suddenly appear. Life is likely to have a different pace and may involve contact with fewer people on a daily basis. All of this needs to be recognised, otherwise it may seem for the person that their life is falling apart. Retirement clearly brings a great deal of time to be filled. Some may have a lifetime of interests and hobbies to draw on to keep up their need for new challenges. Others may have commitments to care for family or friends which increase and take over what was work time. For those who retire with partners there may be new adjustments to be made. Retirement may herald the first time in many years that a couple have had such a sustained period of time together. It may be a testing time for relationships. Some people may find that the focus of their lives together has been their children and not themselves. Couples may need to renegotiate what pattern their lives will take, perhaps for the next 30 years. Everybody knows about the husband who is at home all day getting under his wife's feet. This can be a real problem which causes tensions to emerge in the marriage. Many marriages thrive on periods apart. Retirement, particularly if it goes along with ill-health, may place great strains on a relationship.

For people from black communities, retirement can be a further isolating experience. Some may continue to work within their families, taking on responsibilities to look after grandchildren or to care for other members of the family. For many who have been used to having a great deal of contact with others throughout the day, possibly because their work had been in a factory or workshop setting, retirement can mean seeing fewer people and being on one's own for long parts of the day. Many people may want to take the opportunity to get out of the home again and to meet with others. Day care services or linking people into existing groups and associations may be just what is needed. Social workers need to give attention and understanding to the expectations that older people from other cultures may have, with regard to the respect they feel is due to them as an elder of their community. Some people may expect that their age and life experience, and therefore wisdom, will be acknowledged and revered by younger members of the community. This would have been the case in their country of origin, where they may have turned to elders for guidance and advice when they were young. Older people may feel disappointed or without a role if this turns out not to be their experience now that they are the elder.

Some people continue to do paid work either full-time or part-time once beyond retirement age. For many the motive remains money, particularly if family circumstances are that their partner is not yet retired or that they continue to have family commitments. Continuing with work, even if only on a part-time basis, can also provide a regular weekly activity to help give shape to an individual's life.

Feeling old

Retirement from work places people in a new category. Once people are retired they are seen by the world as old. This is a label that a great many are not ready for. It may not reflect how they feel or indeed, how they see themselves. Hard though it may be to believe, being old can come as a surprise for some people. Miss Ford although 85, always claimed that she did not feel a day over 21. She certainly did not see her view of the world to be any different today than it was when she was 21. She had noticed a little stiffness but not much else. Miss Ford had somehow always thought that she would know when the time had arrived, when finally she was old. She was most surprised to be 85 and still feeling 21. The label of 'old' can be a difficult and frustrating barrier for some people. It can stop them seeing their lives as useful and vital. It can fuel the idea that now is the time to slow down. It may cause them to review or modify their behaviour in light of their age and so begin to act in a manner that they feel is more in keeping with being old. There are, of course, no clear roles of behaviour that belong to the old or to the young. You are who you are and feel what you feel, no matter what age. Social workers will find themselves having to take up this war cry on a regular basis. It is important that we question the services and resources available to older people in order to ensure that what is available offers valid choice to the older person and does not merely conform to someone else's idea of how older people should spend their time.

Miss Ford, like most people, did not give much consideration in her younger years to thinking about what life might be like as an old person. If considered at all, the dream may have been of whiling away the days digging the allotment, or taking long holidays to visit family and friends. There might be a concern about ill-health in the future or inheriting mother's arthritis. But for the most part these will be individual worries that may or may not be part of the future. Talk to any grouping of older people and a number, like Miss Ford, will make reference to feeling and thinking now as they have always done. Few of us would believe that we will radically alter our thoughts and ideas because we have become older. Old age does not bring with it the advent of a new personality and a desire to wear crimpolene skirts. If social workers can know this, then part of our task is not to fall into the trap of consigning old people to the stereotypes we see in daily use. The social work task is to focus on people as individuals and to take on the battles that may be necessary to combat the ageism of others.

Some of this ageism is carried by older people themselves. Part of what people feel about themselves may be because they have been fed negative messages about old age. If people are constantly presented with ideas about how difficult this time can be, with ill-health and loss at every turn, then old age will become a very stressful time. We need to be imaginative in assisting and encouraging individuals to see the possibility of a variety of lifestyles. If someone likes to play bridge it may be more appropriate to find a volunteer to take them along to a bridge club, than to get them a place at a day centre and hope that they will be offered a game of cards.

Ageism

Ageism is rife in many institutions in western societies. British society has a major youth bias that operates in nearly all areas of life. Magazines endlessly focus on how we should all try to look younger. Cosmetic companies spend millions each year to produce creams and lotions that will stop skin from ageing. Getting older is seen as something to worry about and maybe even fear. A view of young is best, old is worst, when promoted at every turn, also has the effect of polarising views and influencing how these age groups see one another. The popular negative view of old age is bound up with how our society views and portrays this period of life. Being old can be seen as having many derogatory connotations. Indeed the term 'old' is often used when someone wishes to put another person down, for example calling someone a silly old fool. People who use these phrases see old age as something apart or different from them. They may see old age as a time when things begin to fail – a person's health, their mental capacities etc. Old people are often labelled as stuck in their ways, unable to take on new ideas or as increasingly rigid and difficult. However, it is our contention that some of these characteristics are well established in an individual's personality long before old age becomes a factor. For example those who live alone, at whatever age, have ample opportunity to get set in their ways. It would be an enlightening exercise for any of us to think about our own interesting everyday little quirks which might be characterful now, but at 70 would be seen as eccentric and cranky.

The power of these stereotypes and generalisations is quite staggering. They are well illustrated by one enterprising social worker who went to talk to some teenagers about the needs of older people. In order to get started, each student was asked to answer ten questions to show what they knew about being old. The answers were, of course, fascinating. A number of these 13-year-olds saw 45 as old, they guessed the pension to be about £100 a week, and complained that old people were smelly and deaf. The social worker then went to an old people's home to ask the residents to answer similar questions but with regard to teenagers. She did not have the nerve to present the information taken from the children, since it was all so negative.

The big surprise came, however, when the school children read what old people had to say about them. They did not see themselves as always screaming and walking in gangs along the pavement. They did not know that old people were constantly afraid of being knocked over by them. Indeed, they were very shocked by just how frightened some of the older people were of them. The teenagers wanted immediately to visit the old people to say that they were sorry that they had felt so scared. This exercise showed very clearly how easy it is to make generalisations about what we expect people to be. Many of the perceptions that both parties had of one another came from images on television and through stories in the newspapers.

Part of the reason that such ideas and generalisations seem to spread may be because many people do not have contact with old people to counter these notions with positive experiences. With the mobility of populations some younger people may grow up without the close contact of grandparents and older family members. For some, their only experience of older people may be those they see on television. The media and most often television has a large role to play in creating our images of older people. We can all think without too much difficulty of established 'old' characters who support some of these general views. Alf Garnett and, in more recent times Victor Meldrew, have fixed firmly in our minds the cantankerous, bad tempered intolerant older man. Women fare equally badly. Phyllis from Coronation Street and Beverley from Desmond's are respectively, man crazy and foolish. Both characters are in a large part amusing because they are old. If they were played as 30-year-olds the storylines would not carry nearly the same punch.

Social services departments are not immune from the ageism which abounds in the rest of society. This can be seen in some of the insensitive planning that goes on. Planners often work on whole populations and make major assumptions about the needs of older people. They assume that people over 85 are all vulnerable and conversely that younger older people do not have needs. They then plan day care on the basis of the location of very old people since they assume there will be high levels of disability and dementia. But in an area of younger older people with traditions of smoking and poor diet there may be an urgent need for day care for people who have had strokes.

Ideally planning should be based on the aggregation of assessments of individual needs; a process it was thought would follow from the priority the assessment process was given in the Community Care legislation. In reality this does not seem to be happening. Understanding the necessarily crude nature of planning and some of the ageist assumptions on which it is based makes it imperative for social workers to feed their perception of need to planners.

For those requiring long term care the same is also true. Bulk provision is always likely to ignore individual needs. Nowhere is this more obvious than when you try to find a place for a younger person with dementia, for example, a person with Down's syndrome and dementia or with early onset Alzheimer's disease. They are plainly unsuited to the normal run of residential homes, yet often there is no alternative. A flexible range of services is needed and we are often best placed to advise on what these might be.

It is not just planners, who are relatively far from the individual users, who use ageist stereotypes. Social workers as individuals are not above bouts of ageist behaviour. As with any other kind of prejudice, it is useful to reflect on practice and to be fully aware of one's own feelings about old age. These may be confused and complex. Some people will have been traumatised by grandparents when a child, others may have been smothered. Current experience also affects our views of old age. For example, how many workers have contact with older people outside their work context? If we do not have a positive experience of older people in our lives, we run the risk of seeing all older people in the same way that we see those with whom we work. Social workers usually have contact with old people and their families when they are bound up in some kind of crisis. If this is the only experience workers have, it can be possible to develop a view that old age is in the most part about disabling and difficult times.

In listening to older people talk about their lives, workers can also begin to feel sad and disappointed for those whose lives appear to have left them unfulfilled. Older people, like the rest of us, have good and bad experiences in their lives. Many of the events they have experienced may not be seen by them as significant until they are reflected upon in later life.

That reflection may take place for the first time when they have begun to talk to a social worker. These may be painful topics for workers to hear about. The loss of a child 40 years ago or the disclosure that a marriage was never truly happy, may leave workers feeling despairing of a life that seems wasted. We need to empathise with the individual but steer clear of the trap of seeing all older people as downtrodden and as victims of their past.

There is, of course, an added danger to be guarded against. In feeling such concern for the older people we work with, we can reinforce negative stereotypes by taking on well meaning but ultimately patronising opinions. One service provider sitting in on a residential admission panel heard a social worker attempting to secure resources for the person she was working with, by constantly referring to her as a 'lovely little old lady'. The social worker was unwittingly promoting the idea that this woman should be helped because she was always grateful, presented no problems and was therefore in some way deserving. We must hope that this was an unthinking statement on the worker's part. Otherwise we must assume that the bad tempered and unattractive 'little old ladies' are not to receive assistance.

We need to be very mindful of what some of our language can convey. A kind of unthinking stereotyping that portrays older people as helpless victims of their situations is a serious kind of ageism. There are good reasons why there can be a tendency to see older people as helpless. If someone is in distress or has difficulty in communicating their wishes, it can be all too easy to fall into a pattern of making decisions over that person's head. The danger is that this kind of thinking leads to poor practice. Sometimes the older person is not consulted because the worker feels they know from previous contact what the individual would wish to do. Often it is more a matter of convincing the older person that it was the right decision after the event. All of this may be done unknowingly and in the best interests of the individual, but it clearly has the effect of taking power and control away from that person.

To help bring home these issues, it can be useful for us to think about how we would wish to be treated in the same situation. Many of us having visited an old people's home to arrange for an admission, have come away saying that we would never

be able to live in such an establishment. We might, for example want more privacy than is offered. If it would not suit us,
maybe the question to be asked is, does it really suit the person we are working with? We need to think through why this
might be acceptable for the individual we are working with,
while not acceptable for ourselves. Is it an issue about poor
choice in services or is it about a view of what older people
can expect and deserve? If it is about choice, then community
care should encourage us to do something about it, such as
raising the issue within the team, or feeding information to
those involved in policy and planning. If it is based on the
view that a poor service is all an older person has a right to
expect, then ageism needs to be acknowledged and challenged.

Teams may wish to know where local Pensioners Associations
or Forums may be located. They may be able to offer a service
in supporting and advocating for older people faced with making
important decisions. They may also be in a position to monitor
ageist practice or policy where they might identify it, for example
by being involved in consultation discussions over community
care plans and development of new services.

A positive view

One of the best ways for us to tackle these ageist issues is, of
course, to focus on the positives that come with being older
and on positive role models. Thankfully there are a great many
examples of older people being active and interested. We may
want to promote these examples with our colleagues and with
older people with whom we work. Almost anything can and
should be possible when you are old. Much of the 1993 European
Year of the Older Person activity was a testimony to this. The
year, launched by the European Community, sought to celebrate
old age and so show that age is not a barrier to having a good
time. The aim was to win respect for older people and to fight
the insecurities and isolation that many older people feel. The
year saw the development of wellbeing programmes, events and
conferences highlighting the needs of older people and a wide
range of arts and sports programmes. All parts of Britain saw
activity. One in Glasgow was A Time of Your Life Exhibition,

which allowed organisations to showcase what they have on offer for older people. A regular event for the last four years in Glasgow has been a three day display by Strathclyde University's Learning in Later Life group. This group has a wide and varied series of events, courses and classes for older people wishing to polish up skills or take up new challenges. We think most social workers would enjoy a book called *Growing Old Disgracefully* (Cooper *et al.*, 1992), which was produced by a group of women who feel that age 55 is the time to take up new challenges and discover who you are.

Some interesting work undertaken in 1993 was an audit across all 12 member states to uncover views from older people on how they felt about being old and what this description meant to them. The Ages and Attitude Survey (Commission of European Communities, 1993) gathered together a great deal of interesting material. An early piece of information gleaned was that people wished to be described as either 'senior citizens' or 'older people.' Of those questioned, 58.1 per cent chose these terms, with elderly, one of the least favourite, only acceptable to 6.6 per cent of those questioned. We need to take on board the fact that older people found the term 'elderly' a negative and dehumanising label. 'Senior citizens' was felt to be positive and 'old' or 'older people' felt to be a descriptive term that placed people in the society in which they lived and did not distance them from it. Of the UK participants questioned, 21 per cent felt that being older had given them a new lease of life. For many of this number, being older meant freedom from work and family responsibilities and with time to enjoy themselves. However, opinions also abounded that older people wanted to be included in social pastimes outside the family. They wanted to share time with people with whom they have something in common, other than their age. It should not be a surprise that it is often more meaningful and apt to see individuals in relation to their interests rather than their families. On this theme there is a very interesting range of old people's homes in Southern California. People are placed according to hobby. So, there is a home for golfers, one for bridge players and another for gardeners. As can be gathered, anyone choosing to live in any of these homes immediately has some common ground with the other residents and an excellent starting point for friendships.

Of course maintaining a positive attitude about ageing may be difficult for some. If the retirement years also bring poor health and disability older people may struggle to see the opportunities to live the life they would like. As Scutton points out in his book *Ageing, Healthy and in Control* (1992), worries about the future and the advent of disease can have a very depressing effect on an individual's outlook. A useful book to recommend to older women who may want to understand how the ageing process is affecting them is *Ourselves Growing Older* (Brown and Siegal 1989). Such information can help to inform people what might be ahead and in this way help them to prepare for their old age.

The view that things will only get worse causes many people to withdraw into themselves seeing little opportunity for pleasure and interest. This may also be a factor for older people from black communities. It may not be until they reach old age that the degree of their difficulties in feeling 'outside' the wider community become truly apparent. Feeling old and as if you do not belong, can only reinforce powerful feelings of isolation and loneliness.

Older people as volunteers

One way that older people will have to address some of this negative thinking can be through their involvement in volunteering. Volunteering can offer an older person the chance to feel busy and useful. Older people have long been active as committee members with tenants associations, within Workers Education branches and in a host of other community based and voluntary groups. Many are involved in providing direct hands-on services to those in need of assistance either as volunteer drivers or as good neighbours and befrienders. They run many of the services that more isolated older people are reliant on to provide them with a good quality of life. The Dixon Halls Community in Glasgow, for example, relies on over 400 older volunteers to run a wide variety of home visiting and good neighbour schemes for a very large population of housebound and disabled older people. Volunteering can also provide an opportunity for older people to establish new networks and friendships with others who share their interests or areas of concern.

We should always have an eagle-eye open, when visiting older people, for the potential volunteer that may hide within. Everyone will have something they can contribute. It may just be that they have not recognised this as a possibility. Offering help to others by being a volunteer is something that should be open to every older person. It is not just an activity for the very fit. In some situations the encouragement to give something back by volunteering may work in a therapeutic way. We should be aware of the need to offer individuals an opportunity to help someone else. It can be very difficult to be constantly on the receiving end of the help of others. Volunteering is very much a feel-good activity and this may be the medicine that some older people need most. Mrs Wilson had been very lonely since her husband died. Although he had dementia he had always been able to be her legs, to go to the shops and get the paper in the morning. She did not go out as she suffered from agoraphobia. Mrs Wilson received a home help to undertake her shopping and chores, but she still missed the caring she had provided for her husband. The social worker involved quickly recruited Mrs Wilson's baking skills to provide scones once a week for the day centre her husband used to attend. Mrs Wilson's wellbeing improved greatly once she had a weekly commitment on which to focus.

As well as recognising that older people can be volunteers, social workers should think about how they might use volunteers to help in the work they do with old people with disabilities. The involvement of volunteers might just be the solution to situations that call for more imaginative problem solving. In one area office, two social workers based in different teams, started a conversation over coffee that led them to discover that between them, they were visiting four people in the same block of flats. The social workers set aside time to visit the flats and do some door knocking with the other tenants. This uncovered one other older person in need of some support. However, as intended, it also produced a couple, themselves recently retired, who took on the good neighbouring of the other five older people. The two good neighbours had noticed some of their neighbours having difficulty but had always felt shy about offering to help for fear of giving offence. These neighbours were, within a couple of years, running a tenants club offering informal day care to older people in their scheme.

Some people feel hesitant about putting themselves forward to offer help, but when asked are only too happy to respond. Some social services departments make wide use of volunteers in a number of different settings. They have a clear policy for recruiting, training and supervising volunteers and clearly see the value in what volunteers can offer. However, if this work has not been developed, it may be worth both individually and in teams, thinking about how they could develop the use of volunteers in supporting the old. Keeping active by being a volunteer can open up a lot of interest for older people. It also encourages people to see themselves in relation to their ability, rather than constrain themselves by seeing and thinking about themselves in relation to their age.

Older people as carers

We are very likely to meet older people as volunteers, but we are certain to meet them as carers. The majority of older people, who require it, are actively cared for by family and partners. Significant numbers of older people are carers themselves. Of the 6.8 million carers quoted by the National Carers Association over 13 per cent are aged over 65. Some of that number will be lifetime partners but a great many will also be neighbours and friends. Caring is a tough physical and emotional task. Carers who are themselves older, are much more likely to experience health and fatigue problems due to the demands of providing care. The caring one partner does for the other may also go unrecognised, confined as it is within the home. Indeed some older people may not welcome the offers of help a social worker, who is outside the family, may want to offer. A visiting son or daughter may have contacted the department feeling that their parents should have help, even if the older people themselves do not want this. We need to negotiate our involvement in this kind of situation with a great deal of tact and diplomacy. It may be that for a while the carer's support is offered to the son or daughter so that they can support their parents.

In getting involved in work with carers we need to acknowledge the emotional support we may need to give, in addition to taking on the task of arranging practical support services. This needs to be done tactfully and with full regard to the effort and commitment of the carer. We may see a clear need for a period in respite care. But this must be recognised alongside the difficulties this may cause both parties. It may be, for example, the first time a couple have ever been apart. This may not seem like a significant worry but, for those experiencing it, it can be very frightening. Much reassurance may need to be given about the care being offered to the partner who is going to be away from home. Special arrangements may need to be made so there can be frequent contact. In such a situation it may not be helpful to advise carers to stay away and have a break while a partner or loved one is in care. This could be taken to suggest that the new care arrangements are better than those provided by the carer and that their input is no longer needed. Some people clearly need to have a 'holiday' together in order to give the carer a break without worry.

Where there is a physical dependence between couples there may be worries about what will happen when the fitter of the two can no longer cope. If the caring relationship breaks down through the ill-health of the carer, a major disaster for both parties can quickly follow. Mr Liddle had cared for his wheelchair bound wife for over five years, when he was admitted to hospital with pneumonia. His wife could not be left at home alone so had to be found a place in a residential home. Finding beds for both of them delayed admission by a week. During this time Mr Liddle's condition deteriorated and he subsequently died 12 hours after his hospital admission was finally achieved. Although Mr Liddle cared for his wife, he saw this undertaking as part of the commitment he made to his wife when they married. He saw it as his job to care, but he did not find the term carer an easy one to accept.

Some older people may not like the title we give them in this respect, as it can imply that they have no other identity, only a role in relation to the person they care for. The title may also cause some difficulty because it was not a role chosen by the individual. This role needs to be checked out with carers. There should be no assumption that the partner or relative on the spot wishes to or is able to provide care. As part of our assess-ment, we should be looking at the relationship between the carer and the cared for. A rocky relationship, or one where couples tend to lead separate lives, may be thrown into crisis when a caring role has to develop.

In some situations the necessity for one partner to provide intimate care for another may be a difficult and uncomfortable situation for both. Issues such as nudity and body functions may be very uncomfortable for some people who have never seen one another unclothed. It is a notion some workers may find very hard to understand, but may be a very real problem for those facing this prospect. In such a situation we need to work hard with other service providers to secure services to take on these tasks and so relieve the worry that such a problem may be causing. We have many useful roles to play in helping individuals negotiate all of these new and troublesome hurdles.

Change and adjustment are what being old is all about. Having to carry a label and be old if you only feel like a 20-year-old will be tough. Having to accept a life without work and therefore without a role will be hard for many. Having to look to a future where ill-health of some description is a likely feature, will bring added problems. The question we need to be thinking about now, is how can social work help with each of these? For those who are fit and well or who are newly retired, contact with a social services department may not be a feature of their lives. If social workers do come across the young old, it is probably because they are active as volunteers or carers. We will be in touch with young older people, who are facing up to new responsibilities of being a carer. We will be assisting them to make the adjustments this calls for and to come to terms with what the future may hold.

For the most part social workers are much more likely to have contact with older people, those who have developed health problems or who are restricted due to disability. For the old old, loss is likely to be an increasing feature in their lives. Loss of networks, partners and others can mean facing life alone and/or adjusting to a dependence on strangers to provide much needed help. There is a helpful role that we can play at almost every stage of adjustment. This is particularly so when change is sudden and major, for example sudden ill health or the death

Flor

of a carer. In this kind of circumstance, we will almost certainly be involved in helping to secure practical resources as well as providing emotional support and assistance to help the individual regain control of their lives and to live with their new situation. This work makes great demands on social workers. It calls for stamina and an ability to cope with a fair degree of stress. But the traffic is not all one way. We have a lot to gain from contact with older people. Some older people come through a crisis such as widowhood and blossom into new individuals who are able to tell us how much they appreciated our help. Team discussion about older people can provide opportunities to learn about listening, supporting and getting underneath complex family relationships. In our contacts with older people we can learn much from people who have lived through interesting and unimaginable times and who are still able to give and help others.

4

Getting Started – Issues in Social Work

Those just getting started in this area of social work have a lot of knowledge and skills to acquire. Often it can feel as if this must be done against the clock. Such is the demand for community care assessments, new workers can sometimes be expected to pick up a caseload and be out visiting almost as soon as they arrive. This expectation is in part fuelled by the belief of some managers that social workers will immediately have all the skills necessary to deal with the particular needs of a wide range of care groups. This will rarely be the case. Not everyone can know everything. Knowledge and skills need to be encouraged with help from other team colleagues and by a suitable induction process. Some social services departments will provide an introductory period for new members of staff. This may take the form of a protected caseload for their first six months or year. Others may have an induction programme arranged, so that new workers shadow a colleague for a short while in order to become familiar with the resources, key colleagues and organisations in the local area. What does not happen nearly often enough is that workers are encouraged to undertake visits with other team members and so have the opportunity to see different approaches in action. Often the most useful skills are picked up as tips from other workers. If you are a new worker starting out, ask to do joint visits and get a feel for how others work. If a formal induction process is not available in your place of work, take the initiative and work something out for yourself. Most colleagues are happy to share what they know. However, because social work is such an individual activity, in that contact with people is just between the social worker and the individual, colleagues can be reluctant to offer advice unless you make the first move.

The purpose of this chapter will be to offer an introduction to issues and knowledge that new workers will need to address in order to work with older people. We will reflect on the settings from which social workers operate; begin to think about practice and the methods that might be used, as well as look at how workers might organise themselves. We will end the chapter with a look at the body of knowledge that new workers need to acquire in order to equip themselves to undertake assessments.

The hospital setting

Community care has impacted significantly on the organisation of both hospital and area based social work teams. In most area offices social workers are now grouped within teams specialising in work with particular care groups. A typical area office could have three teams of social workers; a child care/child protection team, offenders/juvenile justice team and a community care or adult team. Some social services departments have worked with specialist or part specialist structures for some time. However this has usually applied to work such as fostering, work with offenders/intermediate treatment teams and only very occasionally with adults and community care user groups.

Within the hospital team setting there has always been a mix of specialist teams and generic teams. For example, geriatric and psychiatric units usually have attached social workers; other social workers are linked directly to general wards. The tasks that social workers will be involved in, in either setting, will essentially be the same. Both settings are now involved in, or preoccupied with undertaking community care assessments.

In the hospital setting, we, as social workers can quite often find ourselves involved in the overall assessment process very late in the day. By the time a referral is made to a social worker, everyone else's work may be done. Doctors, occupational therapists and other staff have had contact with the patient and their specialist areas of knowledge used in order to reach decisions. At this stage a final call may be made to the social worker, who has then to action discharge and aftercare arrangements. This places us in an uncomfortable position. We may feel that there is little regard for our skills and expertise. The late timing of our involvement may create delays in providing services, for which we are then held accountable. This will not be the case in all hospital settings but for a great many social workers this will be a recurring experience. In order to combat such difficulties hospital social workers find themselves constantly promoting their role, making sure that others understand what we have to offer and ensuring we take our place as part of the multidisciplinary team. Medical and nursing staff need to understand that we do more than just access services. They need to know the full range of help that social work can offer. It is also important for health staff to grasp the time scales within which we have to operate. A service is not accessed by a worker simply by making a phone call. Time is needed to book and plan the help that may be required and to keep the older person informed of developments. As doctors now also struggle with the need to keep within budgets their appreciation that social work services must do the same may be clearer.

The ward staff involved with Mr Forsyth were very frustrated by their contact with the hospital social worker. They had requested that services be arranged so that he could be discharged to his own home. They found the worker's reluctance to move on this difficult to fathom. There was no reason why the man could not go home and ward staff were quizzical to know why arrangements were not being followed through. They did not see, or possibly understand, the behind the scenes work that the social worker was putting in with Mr Forsyth. The social worker knew that a home help could be arranged, but also that there was a good chance Mr Forsyth would dismiss the home help the first time she came to visit him. He had done this previously following other admissions. The social worker put in time to involve and introduce Mr Forsyth to his new home help, to establish a relationship before discharge took place so that his acceptance of this service had more likelihood of success. This process delayed discharge by two days and meant the worker had to fight almost hourly battles to convince ward staff of the necessity of this work.

In theory such a struggle should be less commonplace in

the late 90s. Health and social services authorities are required to develop discharge protocols, sometimes known as discharge agreements. The protocols should spell out the different roles and responsibilities of health and social services staff. In Scotland one such agreement covers the following areas:

- notification of hospital admission
- arrangements for screening for assessment
- identification of 'triggers' for different levels of assessment
- arrangements for notifying the participation of agencies in the assessment process
- criteria for convening formal multidisciplinary meetings
- format for agreeing discharge packages
- arrangements for securing discharge
- arrangements for monitoring the process

Agreements are not sufficient in themselves. It is nurses, social services staff and doctors that have to make them work, but having an agreement to fall back on in times of strife can be useful for the social worker. Nurses are in a key position to improve discharge planning and procedures for patients returning home from hospital; hospital discharge schemes that can mobilise the home care service are an important part of the social work response.

If readmission is necessary, consideration can then be given to how this is handled. Social workers can and do, have a role at the readmission and even the preadmission stage. One geriatric unit always ensured that a social worker was available to go out on a domiciliary visit with the consultant whenever this was requested. In some instances this early involvement made it possible to treat people at home, with medical, nursing and social work resources going in to manage the person, where they chose to be cared for. Depending on the type of unit or ward, there may be opportunities for workers to have some longer term involvement with those who have been discharged. This may mean a useful role in feedback information to the unit and organising the planned readmission, should this be necessary.

A useful booklet for all hospital based workers is the *Hospital Discharge Handbook* produced by the Department of Health

(1994). This is a work manual for nurses, doctors and social workers to examine issues about discharge practice. It is helpful in assisting workers to think about all stages of the discharge process from preadmission through assessment and treatment, to discharge and follow up. It may help to suggest that ward or unit meetings look at this booklet and discuss its contents. If staff can meet together like this, when they are not in the midst of planning a discharge, a helpful examination can take place of each other's pressures and difficulties.

As well as planning for discharge, there are some guidelines or protocols for other professions which can be helpful in clarifying responsibility. The British Geriatric Society's *Guidelines for Collaboration between Geriatric Physicians and Psychiatrists in the Care of the Elderly* (1978) is an attempt at ensuring clear medical responsibility is taken for an individual's care. In terms of treatment, old people often need both medical and psychiatric attention. Yet services demand that they be labelled one or the other. If very unlucky, people can end up being passed between the two services and so not receive appropriate treatment. A more recent Royal College of Physicians publication, *Ensuring Equity and Quality of Care for Elderly People* (1994), covers some of the same issues in relation to doctors working in geriatric medicine and general medicine and gives a host of recommendations as to how acute and specialist services should be managed. Guidelines can be of help in some situations and serve to remind doctors of what their professional organisations have advised on their behalf.

A second issue for hospital based workers, is the divided loyalties we can experience between the need to be part of the multidisciplinary team and our need to establish a social work identity, as part of the social services department. Hospital social workers are geographically nearer to the hospital team and have contact with their medical and nursing colleagues on a daily basis. But social work is our identity in terms of who we are and the principles that govern and guide our actions. As hospital based workers we can find life easier if we forge whatever links we can with area based teams. Hospital social workers are usually in daily contact with area social services offices to secure resources and pass on information about imminent discharges. If the hospital systems mean that contacts with area teams is invariably late or sometimes after a discharge has taken place, then misunderstanding or unhappiness about each other's performance will abound. Hospital based workers may in such a situation feel that they are being squeezed from both sides. If this is the case then action needs to be taken. It may be useful to convey some messages and information in person. There is nothing better than face to face contact. Visits to the area office provide a chance for both sets of social workers to at least see one another. Communication is always easier once you have met and shared a coffee break. It may be worth a hospital team thinking about doing a regular coffee session for area team colleagues. Likewise area team social workers can take opportunities to follow up someone who goes into hospital. The older person will often appreciate the continuity of seeing the same person and the worker will be able to share vital information with those who are now caring for the older person. As area team social workers we should make sure we get invited along to hospital based case discussions. As well as helping with planning for an individual's needs, it is possible to make useful contacts that can be called on in the future. In addition, meeting with hospital colleagues can be a useful way of picking up general knowledge and information about health problems. It is also clearly an opportunity for workers to find out about each other's pressures and constraints.

Participation in hospital discussions provides an opportunity to let medical colleagues, in particular, know the limits to the areas of work social workers can take on, both in terms of what we can offer and in terms of what is not appropriate. Without recognising it we can sometimes end up as a general run around person. We become the worker who picks up any task or responsibility for which other professionals do not have a remit. We need to be straight with health colleagues as to what are the legitimate areas of work for us to address. Learning to say no or that you cannot help may help others to develop, for themselves, the general problem solving skills they expect of us.

The area team setting

Area team social work is different in that the pace, setting and production of results is firmly in the hands of the responsible worker. Once work is allocated to an individual worker the plan of involvement and timing of this are for the social worker and line manager to decide. Some departments will have set timescales for the completion of community care assessments. This can be anything from 21 days, 28 days or longer. Whether it is for the assessment period or longer term work, we are usually thinking at the outset about how much time and in with what frequency, contact needs to be offered. There is often time in an area office setting to work at the individual's pace.

Misunderstandings and different attitudes to time are a source of considerable aggravation. It is almost always worth being clear by which date an action will have been taken, and expecting colleagues in other agencies to do the same.

A major area of development for area based workers is the development of information giving services. There is a duty to provide information about services enshrined in the NHS and Community Care Act. In many areas this is seen as a responsibility covered by public relation sections or by those at a more senior management level. However, it is not sufficient for departments to provide a leaflet explaining what community care is about and leave it at that. It is the job of area teams to see that people understand the information given to them and that they are encouraged to use this information in order to make decisions and choices for themselves. If social work teams look at informing the public about what they do, they can undertake some real preventive work. People in hospitals or who have contact with another professional worker can be said, by and large, to have made it through the barrier to securing help. By being in touch with knowledgeable workers they have a great deal more chance of having problems and difficulties picked up and identified. Older people in the community without these contacts, are still outside the system and are therefore reliant on all sorts of informal networks to help them pick up information in order to secure services and resources. Even services that should exist to direct people to information do not always manage this. For example if Mrs Jenkins has managed to successfully claim Attendance Allowance, she cannot always rely on the Benefits Agency to tell her that she might now be entitled to income support via the Severe Disability Premium if she lives alone. If one department cannot provide information on the function and help offered by another section, then older people will really struggle to find out what they are entitled to know.

As teams begin to think of how they can get information about what they do out to older people, they can first look at how accessible or otherwise their offices are. Are social services offices seen as useful places to go? If local offices do not advertise what they can offer, older people will not use them. Older people would not be wholly wrong, for example, in seeing social services offices as places only for people who are having trouble with their kids.

We need to remember that if older people are not sure what help or support might be on offer, their enquiries for help are likely to be tentative and easily discouraged. For example, some may feel that asking for help is a one way ticket to residential care or that if they ask for extra help they may lose their valued home help or that charges for services will be too high. These worries may not appear rational, but that does not make them any less real. Older people need to be given time to express themselves, particularly if they have struggled some distance into an office, they need to be seen that day and not given an appointment to come back. In some more cynical teams appointments are offered in order to bat people away. We do not know if the research has been done, but it would be interesting to know the volume of missed appointments annually in any area team. If appointments are routinely offered in your office, maybe the team should do some research and with the evidence, make the case for additional staff to provide extra duty cover.

If someone does present themselves at a social services office, you can reasonably expect that they have tried all their usual sources of help first. It may have been very difficult for them to come to an office, so their first impression and the reception they receive will have a significant effect on how comfortable they feel about seeking help. Old people brought up in a tradition of self-reliance may feel ashamed of asking for such help.

It may be that they feel they have failed if they have to admit that they can no longer manage. There may be embarrassment because family have failed to provide help and now assistance must be sought from strangers. Worries may stem from the person's own feelings about being a trouble and a nuisance in asking for help. We need to make real efforts to ensure that asking for help is as easy as possible. Some older people find it very difficult to put their precise needs into words. Time and patience is required and we may need to suggest help rather than wait to be asked. For example, if someone obviously has difficulty in walking or sitting, the existence of OT equipment should be mentioned. Or if someone has a number of health problems and lives alone, help with telephone installation and rental might be suggested. Older people cannot ask for things they do not know exist.

The fact that Mrs Penny had to wait five months for her request for respite care for her 95 year-old father to be dealt with was, however politely, blamed on her. She contacted her local area office asking if they would arrange a holiday for her father. She did not know that the appropriate social work speak was 'respite' and that her use of this word would have secured an almost instant response. We are not simply message takers when listening to someone's worries. We need to ask questions and sometimes suggest answers. It may be appropriate to return to a topic a number of times throughout a conversation to check that you have taken the correct meaning from what the person is trying to say or to ask of you. An interesting study by McEwan (1992) asked a number of older people whom they felt should be responsible for providing care. 52 per cent favoured the state, 39 per cent the family and 28 per cent felt people should look after themselves. Such a mixed picture does indicate that some people may have very ambivalent feelings about contacting social services departments for help.

Older people from black communities may find it particularly difficult to make the approach to formal statutory agencies. Some of those who may have immigrated to Britain came to flee tyranny and oppression. They may have a real worry about formal authorities knowing a great deal about them. There could even be a worry that contact from a social worker is in some way a check to establish their immigration status. To combat these worries an older person may wish to have a number of people present during their interview. This should not be a problem for us. There may be some understandable nervousness if we feel we have an audience watching us, but this can be overcome. The older person might have some hesitancy that their language skills are not good or fear that they might not understand what is being said to them in return. We need to take time to explain and to seek help from others who can aid interpretation. It may be useful to ask someone who is at present using services or has in the past to accompany us on a visit to discuss the help being offered. Obviously any linking together of older people in this way would have to be with the permission of both parties and be acceptable to both.

The social worker asked to visit Mrs Khan worried that the lady seemed very nervous and unsure about using day care. A formal interpreter had accompanied the worker on one visit but was not available to make the other times that the worker had set aside for visiting. The resourceful social worker returned to someone she had worked with in the past and asked if she would come along to talk about the day care service her husband used. The worker left Mrs Khan and Mrs Metha to talk together. The two women got on well together and Mrs Metha agreed to accompany Mrs Khan on her first couple of visits to the centre.

The ways in which social workers can let people know what they do are many and varied. A number of ways can be looked at by a team, in order to decide what is right for their area and locality. Information surgeries, leaflet and poster campaigns should all be seen as positive. A team can produce literature of their own, perhaps explaining the local arrangements for community care assessments. Circulated through places of worship and lunch clubs these can reach a wide audience. Alternatively we can make use of local newsletters, where they exist, to include articles on services and resources accessed through the social services department. Many housing departments and housing associations have news sheets that go out to all their tenants on a regular basis. An article in one of these is a sure way to reach a large number of people. We can also promote information about the wide range of services available from our local voluntary organisations, particularly ones that can be accessed directly by the general public. With a little time and effort a small booklet, detailing all of these, can be produced which is equally valuable to staff in a range of agencies and older people alike.

Time and thought needs to be given to the medium used for delivering information. Are leaflets and booklets available in languages other than English? Can recordings on tape be used rather than the written word? In doing our best to produce information we can unknowingly make many assumptions about literacy skills within a population. Having information on tape can solve this problem. Older people may find it much easier to listen to someone talking rather than struggle to read something with tiny print. If workers can be spared to undertake visits to promote their role, a talk, to say a group of tenants in a local sheltered housing complex, gives people a chance to ask questions and maybe make referrals. All information, in whatever forms, needs to be jargon free and in straightforward, accessible language.

We can of course get our message out through others. It is useful for teams to have regular contact with community activists and other workers in their locality. If this is done, they can begin to understand the social work function and can feel comfortable about making referrals. If this happens then other workers will be able to pass on the message that social workers are OK and have a willingness to help. It may be useful to have formal meetings with some workers, say Community Psychiatric Nurses (CPNs) in order to share information on resources and to update each other on their involvement with particular individuals.

We do recognise that social workers do not need to tout for business, there is already plenty to do. However if older people can be informed about the help and support available, it is more likely that referrals will be made appropriately and earlier, and help offered before caring situations have broken down.

Rural locations

For area team social workers the urban or rural environment will a have significant impact on how services are organised and what resources and networks are around for workers and older people to tap into. The social work service will be no different, but some additional skills for more isolated settings may be called for. If face to face contact can only be infrequent because of travel difficulties then other ways of communication may need to be developed. Phone techniques may need to be perfected, as might the need to work through someone else or to use an interpreter. To get some experience of how to make the most of the telephone, it can be worth spending time with a standby or night duty team of social workers to see how they operate.

The Holt family were supported by a standby social worker in keeping a crisis at bay when their mother with dementia was found walking down the street in her village with no clothes on. The worker patiently talked to all members of the family, as well as concerned neighbours. She spoke to each in turn over the phone, encouraging them to express their feelings and asking them to talk and listen to one another's concerns. This worker felt comfortable about using the phone and was able to encourage the members of the Holt family to be equally comfortable about talking about their difficulties, without the face to face contact of a worker. Knowing how to draw people out and keep them talking, knowing how to distinguish emotion on just the sound of someone's voice are all skills that can be developed and used to good advantage.

Working in isolated rural communities can also bring forward opportunities for new and interesting ways of working, either as a team or with colleagues from other professions. Public services are less and less available in rural settings. There are fewer post offices, not as many shops and a general decline in the public transport service. All of these can isolate people and distance them from the services and support systems that should be there to help. It may be more difficult for family to visit or for older neighbours to call on one another, if for example, the bus service is only twice a day. Collecting a pension may only be possible once a fortnight if the distance to the post office is too great to travel. For those in need of practical support, imaginative thought will need to be given as to how to make services accessible in these isolated locations. We should not be afraid to take on some responsibility for developing new services to meet these kinds of needs. Day care can happen in people's front rooms, Good Neighbours can be recruited from the newly retired. Workers in these settings are in a prime position to see the needs of village communities and to look to new and different solutions to problems. We do not have to wait for ideas about service development to come down from on high, we can develop our own. Ideas, especially if jointly developed with other workers, such as nurses or a GP are likely to be seen as more appropriate responses to local needs and therefore to receive support. For those thinking about setting up or developing new services David Clark's book, *Good Neighbours* (1991) provides a step by step guide to setting up a village care group. This book is helpful in its ideas and informs on the experience of how other people have gone about this task.

Starting and stopping contact

As we get started in working with older people, we need to think about our practice. What is our 'style'? How do we organise and plan our time? These issues are very much the good housekeeping of social work and therefore need to be examined and set in place before we run the risk of lifelong bad habits. Seriously considering these issues allows us to present ourselves as ready and fit for the tasks ahead of us. The good housekeeping issues we want to reflect on here include: thinking about time management, how to manage information, how to record and how to select and use methods of intervention. Diving straight into visiting without looking at these will only be problematic. A great deal of social work is behind the scenes work, away from direct contact with older people. It is important that we get these bits right so we are able to do the job effectively and purposefully.

As social workers embark on new pieces of work, we should be striving for a clear idea of what we want to achieve and be thinking about how we are going to go about it. The time needed to undertake an assessment or complete a piece of work will not be known, but workers should be beginning to think about this. The older person may need to be reminded of time scales as the work progresses so they know what is happening and when to expect results. In order to manage time generally, we need first to know how to organise ourselves. As a worker with a caseload of competing demands, time and thought needs to be given to how all the different parts of a week's work will fit together.

We most commonly use our diaries to plan visits and to write reminder notes to follow up work generated from visits. Losing a diary is easily a social worker's worst nightmare. However planning is about more than just keeping track of appointments. We need to know how to prioritise work, weigh up what can be done quickly, what needs to be started first as it takes a little longer to organise, how and when to review, as well as how to dig out new ideas in order to think about alternative courses of action. If we are not sure how long some things might take, team colleagues often know. Time will need to be built in for writing up and making phone calls, as well as any other necessary admin work. If we are not able to reach the nurse or doctor we are seeking it is usually worthwhile leaving a message saying when we will be in again for the nurse or doctor to call back. People constantly missing each other, because they are never in to receive a phone call, can indicate a lack of time planning and forethought. It certainly gives this impression. If it seems really difficult to run someone to ground, we suggest sending them a letter. It may feel more formal than we would wish to be, but at least they will have the information to hand. It might also be worth enlisting the help of a colleague. If for example the consultant is unavailable it may be that the CPN can take the information and pass it on. This all sounds very obvious, and it is, but we are aware of social workers immobilised by exasperation because they have not stopped to work round a problem.

Reflecting on personal style can be helpful. Do I put off difficult telephone calls? Do I always underestimate travel time? Do I hit a blind panic with piles of paperwork and fail to even start? Once failings are identified they can be addressed.

When we are linking into particular resources we must always ask about notice. A hospital social worker will want to provide an early warning to the local home help organiser that Mrs Isaacs will be out of hospital again by the end of the week. We should know roughly how long someone with a chest infection is likely to be kept in hospital, even though a discharge date has not been discussed. By having services ready, we can help influence the timing of discharge and make this a more organised event. We can do a fair bit of work over the phone. Provisional booking of dates for a regular respite arrangement can be taken prior to a visit, for example. Once dates are booked we will have created some breathing space in which to follow up with the necessary paperwork.

A big part of getting organised is to have some way of dealing with the mass of information generated from contacts with older people. Time needs to be set aside for reading, digesting and redirecting information received. It is impossible to be organised if everything we know is in our heads. Information exists when other people can see it. If there are gaps in information, we need to think about how they can be filled. When speaking to a consultant, for example, about the person she saw on a domiciliary visit, it is worth asking for a copy of the letter she will be sending to the GP. This will be useful to have to hand if authoritative reference to medical information is needed for, say, a sudden admission to respite care. It is often worthwhile to ask some service providers to put in writing the information they have delivered over the phone; likewise writing to them about worries and concerns. Sometimes if others see issues spelt out on paper, it helps to galvanize them into action.

We do not want to suggest that being organised is about cutting corners or establishing plans into which older people then have to fit. What we are wanting to emphasise is the value of thinking ahead by taking time to think through the consequences of the situation and thinking of issues that may need looking into later. If, for example, someone asks for respite care in June, it is worth suggesting they think about another set of dates towards the end of the year. Or if an older person has dementia, it can be useful to ask the line manager to timetable an update referral in six months time with the home help organiser when the person's functioning may have changed. All these issues are about staying on top of the work and providing a sensitive, thoughtful service. A very useful book for looking at personal management is Pedlar and Boydell's *Managing Yourself* (1985). It provides a clear outline of the stages of decision making and can be an aid in helping to prioritise and clarify the aims of work. If paper is a problem, Declan Treacy's book, *Clear Your Desk* (1991) is essential reading. His book makes useful points about the distractions unfinished paperwork can cause. He also points out that people spend on average 22 minutes each day just looking for things in and around their desks. One of the simplest ways to take control is to make clear decisions about any paperwork passing through our hands. There are four choices: you can do it immediately, do it later, pass it on or bin it. Treacy's book helps to get us thinking about how to organise ourselves and keep paperwork to a minimum. Being organised is also about personal safety. When signing in and out from an office always tell people where you are going. Instead of just 'visits, back at 4.00pm', put the names of those you are going to see. At least then if you do not return, your colleagues will know where to start looking.

In getting ready to go out visiting we need to give some consideration as to how we present ourselves. This means looking clean and cheerful. We all have off days. In our experience these are days for filing or writing up notes rather than visiting if it is possible to rearrange plans. Visiting when you have no mental energy can be a disservice to an older person who may have been looking forward to the visit. She may even blame herself when the visit is flat and there is no rapport.

Stopping and thinking before dashing out to visit can make the visit itself more useful. What might the older person be expecting? What might be the issues of sensitivity to particular cultural or religious observances that the worker will need to respect? This may mean not visiting on a prayer day or during religious holidays. We need to be sure that all our contacts with old people and their families are constructive and purposeful. As social workers we need to know why we are visiting. This may sound a little nonsensical, but a number of social workers find themselves calling to see people, their only thought being that the individual is 'due' a visit. They may not have visited for a while, so may not be up to date with the problems being experienced by the older person. Visits might be with the purpose of monitoring progress but a worker might not have thought through what they intend to be looking out for. These vague and potentially meaningless visits can be baffling to older people and are often a poor use of time.

When we are out and about we need to make sure that we are equipped for any emergencies that may turn up. The phone number of the standby/night duty team may be useful if the call is late in the day. A note of other emergency services numbers in the front of the diary, such as police, gas and electricity contact numbers, can come in handy. On a practical note it can be helpful to carry some of our own resources with us. One social worker always made sure that she had a few dustbin liners in her car. That way, when out visiting an older person who might have problems keeping up a level of tidiness in their home, she could help out by offering to fill a bin bag with rubbish and taking this away for them.

We also need to think at some point of how to disengage. Saying goodbye after a long period of time contact is hard. We may have weathered many storms with an older person and they may have come to rely on us as they would a daughter. Saying goodbye acts as a reminder to both parties that the social worker is not the older person's friend, but someone who has helped to resolve an issue but who is now moving on. This is hard on both parties. The older person may feel they are losing someone they think they will never see again. They may have told us some intimate worries and confidences that we are now carrying away with us. We may feel a real emotional involvement and that we have let the older person down very badly just when they might be needing us, for example after they have gone into care or have ceased to be a carer. Some workers can only untangle themselves if they find another person to hand the individual on to. However this does not always work. Relationships cannot be passed on in this way. Sometimes we walk out of people's lives at times of crisis, and do this unintentionally. We often cease to visit when someone is placed in residential care. This can be just at the time when the older person needs to have a regular visitor coming to see them. If someone has gone into care the chances are that they will have lost a host of callers who used to come to their door every week. With no nurse, home help or driver from the day care centre, the social worker may be the last person to cling on to. The effort to keep some kind of contact will be very much appreciated. If for some reason we have frequent contact with a home, we can provide some continuity in people's lives if we make a point of always giving ten minutes to talk to individuals we placed there. Some people keep a Christmas or birthday card list; a simple way of letting people know that they are not forgotten.

At the stage of saying goodbye, we need to take time to reflect on what we have learned from our involvement. This question can be asked in relation to the direct work with the older person, as well as of the contacts we have had with other colleagues. We can usefully reflect on different approaches that could have been used and who was helpful and who was not. This is the kind of reflection that we often fail to make as much time for as we should.

Using information

The next piece of preparation is the development of a good information system. Once we get started we quickly amass information about useful services and resources. Most people carry round in their heads details about how things work, what services they have found useful and the procedures for securing particular resources. It is important to pool this information so that others can tap into and add to it. Information is one of the tools of the trade. It needs time, thought and effort to make it accessible enough to work for you. Computers are the ideal tool on which to store and record information, but they are still sadly few and far between in social services offices. If computers are not around, there are other methods. The most available system is the card index box. The biggest size box with the biggest cards available is best. Then a classification system is needed. The simplest will be to reference all entries by the service being provided: write on the lugs the possible areas of help like shopping, visiting, home support, laundry service, commodes. Then place cards that detail the agencies that provide this particular help or service in each of these sections. Each agency should have its own card and have recorded the following information: name, address, telephone number, person to speak to, services provided, criteria for eligibility, charge made, geographical area covered and any other notes that seem relevant. A word or two in your own code as to what you think about the service can be useful: a kind of quality assurance note if you wish. The advantages of a box filing system are considerable. When you need to update information, you merely write out a fresh card and throw the old one away. Another advantage is that they are accessible to other workers and unlike sheets of paper do not curl up and go brown. Others may also be able to add to your system when they hear about or visit new services. Getting a system started can be easier when there are resources directories held within the team. It is then much easier to enter information about what look to be relevant and useful services on cards and then update them as they are used, or particular services are accessed.

Services are one thing to record, useful people another: a card, for example, on that wonderfully helpful caretaker that you met when working with Mrs Darcy. He might become a resource to be approached when you are next working with someone who lives in that block of flats. Likewise you might have a miscellaneous category where you keep details on people or organisations who are not resource or service providers, but who might help out on a one-off basis if asked. One social worker invented a resource by walking into a convent situated in the same street as a person she was visiting. Mrs McCrory needed helping into bed each night but had no one she could call on to give her a hand. She would usually sleep in a chair, but this was uncomfortable and she would prefer her bed if only she could get into it. The social worker went into the convent and asked if any of the sisters would help. They immediately said yes and so became a potential resource in the neighbourhood. Not one to be paraded loudly, but one that could be tapped in to when all else failed.

The index box can also be useful as a place to keep notes about procedural information. Information about housing allocation, notice needed by departments for particular services, and criteria for telephone rental can all be recorded. A few useful reminder notes on a card will mean that the information is to hand and this will help speed the response to those seeking such information.

Records and language

Recording

Having thought about personal management and information collection, good recording habits are next for consideration. Recording, keeping case notes, doing write-ups, whatever the terminology used, is the method used for social workers to keep a track of action taken, the development of plans and reviews of progress. In terms of the agency it is also enables line managers to see what is being done and to be able to respond appropriately should action be required during absences. Reading someone's else notes is usually difficult. Aside from handwriting it may be difficult to grasp quickly what has been going on. Those having to respond quickly to a crisis will not have time to read through pages of interesting narrative. Colleagues in a hurry to get information must be able to see clearly factual information such as phone numbers, details of next of kin, and so on and to see the progress of the work undertaken.

We need to think about the style and layout of our written notes. Some kind of uniformity in layout and sequence will be a help to both us and other readers. Without being too prescriptive, we would like here to rough out a style guideline that could help to make information more accessible. The essential purpose of any write-up is keep current the information gathered about an individual, their family and the problems they are experiencing and to record action taken by the worker as a consequence of their contact. These then are the two components to the write-up. We should record who was seen during a visit, what issues were discussed, any additional information gathered and what action is to be taken and by whom. Before listing who was seen or spoken to, it may be useful to record the timing of the contact.

Mrs Parker always seemed reasonably alert and confident when the social worker visited in the morning. The social worker could not understand why the family kept pestering the GP and her office, claiming that Mrs Parker was at risk because she was so muddled. The social worker failed to appreciate that Mrs Parker's mental competence deteriorated as the day went on. By the time of the relatives' visits in the evening she was very confused indeed. Had the social worker recorded the time of her visits this would have assisted her to see when she was calling and so think about varying the time of her calls.

Having recorded factual information in one paragraph, observations of the particular situation need to be recorded in another. Observations are important, but they should be recorded in such a way that a reader looking at the notes can be clear about what is fact and what is observation.

A great many social workers find it useful to record the plan of action once this has been agreed with the individual. In the recording of any plan, tasks should be spelt out, with deadlines and a review set at regular intervals to chart progress. The review may be most usefully written up after discussion in supervision. This summary paragraph can spell out progress or the lack of it. As new information comes in about family or significant other data, for instance names, telephone numbers, this should be recorded on a front sheet, or if in the body of the text, highlighted in such a way that it stands out. If entering information about particular services, a start and end date should be recorded. Some workers, who have coloured pens, use different highlighter colours to make names and phone numbers, time and date of visits stand out. If this seems a little too colourful, important pieces of information can be underlined, so that they catch the eye as soon as someone starts to read. Although a particular file may be open and as such everyone knows who is the key person involved, it is important to initial any written entry. Others who take action from time to time will want to record this, and they too should initial entries so that everyone knows who has been involved.

After a period of working with someone, particularly if it is a complex situation, it can be a useful exercise to write a report. This means writing a report-cum-social history and getting it typed up. Reflecting on what is known, considering the strengths and weaknesses of the individual, and grouping the information, help thinking about patterns and possible solutions. Summing up work in this way can help to focus on some of the more hidden issues. Such a report will also be extremely handy should there be a need to contact doctors, consultants or service providers and to provide them with a clear succinct picture of what is happening at short notice.

The move to community care assessments has seen a growth

in the number of forms social workers are expected to complete. Although forms may carry a lot of useful information, they are not a substitute for good recording. Write-ups may be briefer because a lot of the information is already covered on the forms, but they should still be there, as should reports and reviews. It is often helpful to give the older person information in writing which explains what is being offered. This, often in the form of a letter confirming dates and arrangements, can be accompanied by a sheet of paper which lists the phone numbers of all the people currently providing help. Community care assessments mean that older people and their carers are now being given copies of care plans once they have been set in motion. This can be made available, with the person's permission, to whoever needs a copy. An older person may want more than one copy so they can pass these out around the family to make sure that they know what the care arrangements are.

The final word on recording concerns the language used. Open access to files is now policy in all local authorities. Such a policy should make us think about how we record what we see and do. This does not mean taking a defensive stance, and not recording feelings and observations in case they might cause offence. Instead it should encourage us to think about the kind of language and use of phrases that can be open to different interpretations. For example, terms such as nice, dirty, unkempt and lovely, do not have a place in write-ups. They do not convey any real meaning or description of a situation and they can and do mean different things to different people.

A description of Mrs Martin's flat was provided at a case conference as an attempt to offer some information on how well or otherwise she was managing to look after herself. The social worker suggested that the flat was dirty, and that the kitchen was full of filthy dishes. The warden of the sheltered scheme where Mrs Martin lived, rallied to her defence. She explained that there were some dishes in the sink in need of washing, but that the 'kitchen' was not full. Mrs Martin piled up her dishes so that she washed three days of used dishes at one time. She did this because she found standing at the sink difficult due to her arthritis. The dirty flat, on close questioning, turned out to refer to one upset ashtray which had scattered its contents across a wide area of carpet. Mrs Martin was unable to clean this up herself because she had difficulty with bending. The ashtray had therefore to be left overnight until the home help came the next morning.

We all have different ideas about what is nice or what constitutes dirt. The easiest way around this difficulty is to record exactly what is seen. This may make some write-ups a bit more long winded, but it does mean that people can only take issue with whether they believe what is written, rather than the interpretation. In Mrs Martin's case it would have been better, for example, rather than say the room was filthy, to have written that in the room there was an overturned ashtray on the floor. Everything recorded on paper should be able to be open to discussion and explanation. It does not mean to say discussing everything recorded or observed, but it does mean that if an older person wishes to see their case file we can stand by everything written down. We should at some point in our involvement explain to individuals that they have the right to see their case file. This can help to build up trust, where this needs to be encouraged, as people will see that we are concerned to be open and honest with them. The same can also be said of work with other colleagues and professionals. If they raise an important issue it is worth checking with them that they are aware that we will be recording what they say. In some situations we may write down literally, in quotation marks, what has been said.

We social workers spend a lot of time on the telephone. Jotting down basic facts as people speak is a useful practice. Writing down what they say verbatim can deflect from listening to the tone as well as the words. It is often worth feeding back key points or facts to the other person to make sure there is an agreed understanding. Some people keep a constant notebook for rough notes on all kinds of conversations which they then transfer to records, cards, action lists and so on before crossing them out. This avoids losing the essential piece of paper in the pile on the desk.

Supervision

We are both strong believers in supervision. In our view all social workers should have timetabled throughout their diary a regular slot for supervision. Supervision is a vital part of social work practice. It is crucial time that should be set aside for workers to update line managers and to reflect on daily practice. Getting good supervision is sometimes problematic, but new workers need to be assertive with their line managers and sort out a regular time for this. A standing agenda can be useful so that time is made to look at personal and career development, as well as review cases. It can be important for both parties to work out what value base they share. Are they on the same wavelength about certain practices? If not, how do they accommodate each other's views? Line managers will need to make clear the requirements the department has of each of its employees and within what frameworks they are expected to operate.

The formal supervision session is there primarily for workers to discuss with their managers the work they are undertaking with individuals. Workers may want to check out that their feelings are correct, that they have covered all the possibilities for action and that they have talked to the right people. It is the time to stimulate new ideas, clarify thoughts and examine motives. It may be that in a session, the worker begins by updating the manager on the progress of work so far, this may mean that all work is discussed each time or just a few cases are reviewed so that a detailed discussion can take place. Together plans and developments can be reviewed and decisions made for future involvement. In these kinds of discussion the line manager should be asking workers to reflect on different aspects of their involvement. This will help the worker to think about other approaches, their own feelings and to see the consequences of patterns of action where these emerge. The worker may have to give some time to looking at her own feelings in different situations and may find the line manager can play a useful role in this. Supervision should offer a decision making framework for workers; they can take this time to look at eligibility for services and consider issues of quality in the services they seek to use. Supervision should ideally be minuted so that workers and line managers are clear about agreed courses of action. Minutes can also be reviewed and updated. Supervision is a tool all workers can use at whatever stage of their career development. For those interested in supervision, or who may

be offering this to students or other workers, *Supervision* by
Gambrill and Stein (1983) will prove to be a useful book to read.

Supervision is most commonly held as a session between workers
and their line manager, but there can be variations on this
theme. Teams may want to look at team supervision or the use
of case discussions as a way of passing on knowledge and learning
between a group. However, all involved in using this model
need to be clear about where the responsibility lies for any of
the decisions that may be made after such discussion.

A bottom line

As a final, but vital issue, social workers need to develop as
part of our practice a bottom line. A bottom line should be a
guide to what we feel is and is not acceptable or appropriate
behaviour in any given situation. If a user falls below the bottom
line, then the clear need for intervention becomes apparent.
There may be rules within a team or department as to what is
and is not acceptable but these are, frankly, rare. Workers need,
with their line managers, to think about what constitutes their
cut off point and what it is that would make them think that
action may be necessary when it is not the choice or wish of
the person with whom they are working.

The first time we as social workers knock on a door, we are
likely to think about the physical environment we see in terms
of what might be acceptable to us personally. Once we have
built up experience of seeing lots of different homes and
situations the likelihood is that we will begin to compare
situations and use this knowledge to judge the suitability of a
particular environment. If a worker does not possess a bottom
line, then we run the risk of constantly accepting behaviour or
an environment as different or peculiar to that individual and
so we never reach a time when we see something as unacceptable or inappropriate. We encourage self determination wherever possible, but at some point we also need to stand up and
say that the best interests of the person are not served by the
course of action they wish to choose. In difficult situations such
as this, we need to talk with the older person and their family
in order to try and achieve some level of understanding of

each other's perceptions. Individuals need to know what the boundaries are that the rest of us have to live by and observe.

Mrs Harland and her son James both had long histories of mental health difficulties. They lived under siege from local neighbours and children. All the windows in their house were boarded up and the garden was full of debris. The couple lived only in the front room. They had a number of broken electric fires, two sofas with no cushions which they used to sleep on and three carpets laid one on top of the other covering the floor space. The floor was littered with old food, plates, cups and meals on wheels foil dishes. Two cats and a dog roamed the room. The social worker visited this couple weekly, trying to convince them to have their living space cleaned up. This was always refused. The house and the couple were in a fairly poor state but they would not accept any help. The social worker did not feel it appropriate to tell them how to run their lives and so did not override their wishes. However the worker had as her bottom line the appearance of animal or human faeces. She had agreed with her line manager that if she saw these it would be clearly time to act with or without the consent of the couple. This occasion did arise and having warned the couple that faeces littering their living space would not be tolerated, she overruled their views and arranged for the room to be cleaned. As is not uncommon, Mrs Harland and her son responded well to the care they received and the general cleaning up that took place. Mrs Harland became so comfortable she refused to leave the old people's home that she had agreed to be placed in, once her own home was ready for her return.

This may sound like a rather extreme example. We need lots of bottom lines for lots of different situations. It may even be a specific decision for each situation. In order to think through all the possibilities for action, colleagues and line managers can advise on the use of public and mental health legislation and to what degree other possibilities for compulsion might be used.

Sources of advocacy for people who cannot speak up for themselves are also useful to determine. It may simply be necessary to find another professional involved such as the CPN. Treating conflicts of interest in an open and above board way can be very helpful for older people and families.

Mrs McKenzie was a widow with dementia who was living at some risk from leaving her home and getting lost. She also troubled a neighbour at odd times of the night. The neighbour was demanding action. In such a situation we need to be clear about what makes us react. Is it someone crossing our bottom line or is it responding to the demands of those being troubled? We should be alert to the possibility that we are taking action because a neighbour complains. This may be the trigger but we need to be sure why we are taking action. In some places a case conference might be called to discuss Mrs McKenzie's situation and to consider the options. In others a meeting of all parties, including relatives and neighbours, can be called to consider a care plan and the contribution of all concerned. The involvement of Mrs McKenzie, with or without an advocate in these discussions, would be a matter of judgement.

Workers involved in managing care plans should be able to arrange these kinds of meetings as they are appropriate. With a care management system in place each agency involved should be clear whom to contact to organise such a meeting. Regular reviews may already be in place with some care management situations.

Having a view about what is and is not acceptable is important, it must also be accessible and understood by co-workers and line managers so that they can share in the making of decisions and in supporting one another. A starting point is to look at any policy statements that may exist about what is and is not acceptable treatment in respect of staff as employees. Staff have a right to expect that the role and the job that they do be treated with a degree of respect, by colleagues as well as those using the service. What is the department's response, if for example, a worker is racially abused by an older person? What action is taken if an older person or a carer physically assaults a social worker? Do the people involved continue to receive a service or is this only offered on condition that they accept the equal opportunities statement of the authority? As well as older people knowing where they stand in relation to us, we need to be clear about what recourse we may have if someone else steps over the line in respect of our needs. Some departments may have policies to deal with such difficulties. These may be reflected in an equal opportunities statement, for example.

Social work practice and methods

Whatever the setting or location from which social work is offered, major methods of working will be held in common. Central to any application of social work methods are the principles of confidentiality and respect for an individual's right to self determination. These values should underpin all social work contact with older people. They should guide the way we conduct ourselves with any individual and in the representations we may make on that individual's behalf to any other agency. Issues of particular good practice may, by contrast, be determined and dictated by the employing agency. Policies which inform practice may be formulated by senior management or may evolve as good practice in area offices. We need to be aware of the latter and be sure to clarify what they mean in practice. Discussion about particular practices can be useful so that new workers can influence what they are being asked to adopt.

Behind the methods highlighted here is good anti-discriminatory practice. Taking account of an individuals's race, religion, age, gender, sexual preference, language, level of disability and culture is good social work practice. We cannot begin our work with older people unless we are able to reflect on each of these issues. The capacity of an older person to address the difficulties they may face is influenced by many issues. In order to be able to look at these, we first need to examine our own motives and actions. When we prioritise our work, do the same individuals always get put to the end of our visiting list? If so, why? How will we react when we visit a home and see very obvious evidence of a particular political or sectarian affiliation which we find personally unacceptable? We may feel compromised in such situations. We may have an internal conflict between knowing that everybody is entitled to help, but feeling we would rather not be the person to deliver it. These are everyday issues which we need to examine and air with line managers.

The teams in which we work should probably take time regularly to see whether all sections of the community are served and if not, why not. We need to be able to see discriminatory behaviour around us. Discrimination can have many layers, it works at individual, institutional and societal levels and is both covert and hidden. We need to be aware of it so that we can then challenge it. This may be problematic for some workers, particularly if the discrimination we identify is from a person using the service. We might be concerned that challenging the views of such an individual may alienate them, or that the relationship we have been struggling to develop will come to an end as a result of taking issue with the older person. It is possible to raise these issues with older people, but it needs a constructive approach by questioning people as to why they think what they think, and whether they understand how their comment can cause offence. Addressing discriminatory statements is a responsibility for all workers.

Mrs Howe was a staunch member of her church. Her home, decorated with religious artifacts, reflected her beliefs. She never hesitated to question all her visitors to find out 'where they stood' in relation to her views and ideas. Any caller not willing to go along with her unquestioningly was quickly shown the door. After two incidents the social worker had to speak to Mrs Howe to explain that although her views would always be respected she could not ask the home help to undertake activities or actions offensive to her personally, for example assisting Mrs Howe to take part in an Orange Walk.

If concerns are about the behaviour of a particular service or work colleague these are best discussed with the line manager. There may be a number of procedural avenues to follow in such a circumstance and we may be asked to formally give evidence or report our concerns.

One of the issues social workers in our field constantly have to face is age discrimination which we mentioned in Chapter 2. We have a responsibility to raise it and to increase awareness about it. Whilst not wanting to take a competitive approach with other groups we need to ensure that older people receive the same level of service. This is not easy. Age discrimination is built into the benefits system for example.

For social workers who have undertaken formal training the term 'social work methods' will be familiar. Methods are our tool kit. They can help us to reflect and plan our work with clear goals. Social work methods are generic in their application. There is no set method for working with older people. However there is a growing body of literature that now reflects the application of particular methods on working with older people. For those wishing to develop particular skills, Alison Frogatt's book *Family Work with Elderly People* (1990) and Joan Cooper's book *Social Groupwork with Elderly People in Hospital* (1980) are helpful starting points in these particular areas. *Dementia: New Skills for Social Workers* (Chapman and Marshall, 1994) is helpful. The book review sections of the *Journal of Dementia Care* and *Community Care* are the best places to find the latest books on methods.

It ought to be the case that the nature of skills and theoretical knowledge social workers apply to their work with old people is dependent on the situation in which they are working. Approaches may sometimes overlap as different circumstances throw up the need for different responses. A task centred approach, for example, stresses clear goals and brief planned work. It helps to focus the worker and the older person on what needs to be undertaken and what is to achieved. It appears very straightforward and may therefore make the most sense to an individual. A clear negotiation takes place around the piece of work to be achieved, tasks are divided between a number of parties and action taken. The goal is the achievement of the task. The task is central to all activity and no other areas of work or concern are up for discussion while the task is being addressed. It is less appropriate in complex situations or ones with a high care management focus. Goldberg, Walker and Robinson (1977) provide a useful exploration of task centred work with older people for those interested in this approach.

The unitary or systems approach as described for example by Pincus and Minahan (1973) is one that has universal application within social work. It focuses on the clear need to bring about change to an individual's life or to their situation. The unitary approach sees change brought about through the use of four systems. The social worker acts as the change agent (the catalyst for change), the target system is the goal or result, the action system is concerned with how the goal is to be achieved and the user system looks at the role of the individual concerned. Within this approach, target systems can be a desired change in behaviour or the exerting of influence on a service or other person. Review and reappraisal are important with this approach as players can change places at different stages on the way to achieving the desired goal. This approach is probably a reasonable description of what social workers do most of the time, although in practice it tends not to be given a formal systems label. It is an excellent tool for analysis rather than a guide to what actually needs to be done.

Crisis work is a method often used when working with older people. When working with people in crisis, we need to listen properly to what is being said. We need to hear the worry and concern in people's voices and be able to respond in a way acceptable to the older person. Crisis work needs lots of time but is essentially short term. We may need to slow things down for the individual and give the person time to express themselves. We may find ourselves to be the only person the older person can really turn to, to confide their worries and fears. A crisis does not have to be a big event that can be easily seen. It may be an internal emotional crisis, that has to be recognised and reacted to. Miss Willis had shared her entire life with her sister Gertrude. When Gertrude suddenly died, Miss Willis's world was shattered. She had no other family to support her and clung for comfort and support to her social worker and home help. To see Miss Willis through this very frightening time both workers needed to provide daily contact with Miss Willis. The giving of this time helped Miss Willis move through this crisis and make a transition to a new home.

Sometimes we have to concentrate to make sure that we understand the crisis and to see this as a new experience for the particular older person. We may have heard a similar worry or story a number of times. We may know that these difficulties can be sorted out and resolved without too much difficulty. However for the older person it is very new and very worrying. Appropriate reactions are important so that the older person can see that their crisis is being taken seriously. In such situations we need to know when to start putting in the extra effort. When in crisis, people may lose the ability to do even the simplest things for themselves. They might need the social worker to step in and sort things out that they would normally be able to manage for themselves. This needs to be done wholeheartedly and without fuss or negotiation. When someone is having a crisis they need to know that they can trust the social worker and that the requests they make are responded to.

Mrs Lee was cared for by her husband until his sudden death.

She was wheelchair bound and had been admitted to hospital when he was taken ill. There was no one else to look after her. Although he died in hospital Mrs Lee wanted her husband to be buried from home and his body returned to the home they had shared for 50 years prior to the funeral. The social worker and the doctors could have easily said no to Mrs Lee and she would have had no choice but to accept this. To the social worker it was apparent that this was Mrs Lee's crisis. She needed to do the right thing by her husband in order to come to terms with her loss. She had not been with her husband since his admission to hospital and she needed desperately to say goodbye to him. The social worker spent two days doing nothing else but making arrangements for Mrs Lee's temporary discharge, organising around the clock care for a 27 hour period and arranging the funeral. Many nurses and medical staff wondered why the social worker was bothering to do all this. But the worker was very clear that Mrs Lee needed to resolve this crisis. She could then plan for her future.

Other approaches open to social workers are bound up within casework techniques, for example, counselling and dynamic interviewing. Counselling is a skilled area of work and not one easily dipped in and out of. Workers interested in this area of work should look at the wide range of material on this method. *Counselling Carers* by Papadopoulos (1993) for example is interesting, since it highlights the stress and role played by prolonged grief amongst carers and how counselling can help to address this issue. Much counselling work is, by nature, a medium to long term endeavour. If this is going to be offered it should be timetabled, with an end negotiated. Any plans to offer a counselling service has time implications for the worker and their line manager. It is also an issue for the older person. Do they wish a counselling relationship? Do they understand what this might mean in terms of the depth of issues to be explored?

Counselling is not always on offer to older people, but it should be. If time is taken, this approach can and does have very satisfactory effects. Mrs Paul worked part time as a home help. She had worked on beyond retirement age, as she had no wish to face being at home and becoming a full-time carer for her disabled husband and brother. Her single brother had come to live with her and her husband 18 months ago after he suffered a stroke. Since this time her husband had also had a stroke. This left her caring for two heavily dependent men. The source of Mrs Paul's concern was that her husband and her brother did not get on. They both made constant claims for her attention. Her husband would not attend the day centre as his brother-in-law already went there. At home they sat in separate rooms and she had to run between them. The student social worker allocated to work with them quickly identified a malfunctioning family. He began to plan a course of counselling sessions to address issues about the relationships within the family. The supervising social worker was sceptical about this endeavour and felt that a range of services to keep the individuals apart and give Mrs Paul a break might be more useful. The student was, however, given support to develop his idea and indeed worked with the trio to achieve some amazing results. Issues of anger, being taken for granted and self-image were opened up and addressed. The family did change; they became friends. They wept when the student left. They all felt they would never have been able to get out of the hole they had dug for themselves without the help of this worker.

Hospital based social workers probably have more opportunity for developing this method of working. They have more direct contact time with individuals, roughly 55–65 per cent, rather than an area team average of 30–35 per cent face to face time (Neill and Williams 1992). Their counselling skills are also more likely to receive regular exercise as they work with people who are coming to terms with the sudden news of disability or terminal illness.

Dynamic interviewing as a method is usually used in short-term focused work with an individual, where the aim is to change set interactional patterns of reacting and behaving. This interviewing technique works on the basis of flipping: changing the negative statements and views made by the individual into positive ones. Information is constantly verified and clarified to assist the individual to become unstuck and see their difficulty from another angle. Those with an interest in this technique should find Mayle's book, *Dynamic Interviewing* (1989) a useful read.

Social workers can also make use of therapeutic approaches drawn from other disciplines. One which has received attention and support from those working in the field of dementia is

Validation Therapy. Validation Therapy is in essence a way of communicating with people who have dementia, by validating and respecting their feelings in whatever time and place is real to them, even though this may not be the correct 'here and now' reality. Naomi Feil's (1982) development of this therapy encourages workers to concentrate on asking 'what?' and 'who?' rather, than 'why?' when an older person seems to be focusing on a past life event. This approach has yet to be researched to any extent but many practitioners are finding it useful.

Another approach that might be of use is Critical Path analysis. This has been a well-known tool for those working in the child care field with families where abuse is an issue. The use of Lynch's Critical Path approach (1976) can offer some assistance to those working with old people who are in the middle of complex relationship tangles. Critical paths allow workers to map out individuals' lives and to see clearly repeating problematic patterns that are continuing into new caring relationships.

Another way of trying different methods and learning new skills is co-working with colleagues. This is not commonplace in work with older people but is a very good way for a worker starting out to pick up on useful skills. Social work activity is on the whole quite a private business. We do not usually encourage others to watch us in action. However it can be very useful. We get to see a different approach and can pick up new skills.

In complex situations co-working can assist individuals and their families, by providing more than one person for them to call on. Workers can either jointly visit or take turns. For someone who might need quite long-term support, a team of workers might be introduced over time. This can also speed response to problems as each member of the team knows the situation and is known to the family. Such an arrangement can work very well provided it is properly negotiated with the older person and their carer. Mrs Jefferys was a regular with an area office intake team. She rang the office most afternoons just to say hello. After her home help left in the morning she found the remaining day very long and lonely. Mrs Jefferys was reassured if she was able to speak to someone in the afternoon. When she was first known to the office she would ring with a 'crisis' so that someone would take the time to talk to her or go out and visit. After numerous phone calls the team agreed that the duty officer of the day would give Mrs Jefferys five minutes every day to talk. Mrs Jefferys was very pleased with this arrangement. She got to know each member of the team and adopted them en masse. She took on the job of worrying about a worker's sick pets and any other little happenings. She also contributed regularly to leaving gifts and birthdays. Mrs Jefferys was managed by the team and she received a service that meant a great deal to her but was easily controlled in terms of the demands it made. In the use of any methods or approaches, time needs to be built in for a review of practice, to see if it is continuing to work. A clear plan with an individual's agreement must always be the starting point.

Self-care

Being a good social worker, unfortunately, does have its pit-falls. Being able to empathise with an individual, to make yourself available to absorb their worries and concerns can and will take its toll. Social work is a very stressful job. It is very difficult to walk away from someone who is in need of help and to know that they will not be getting the assistance they require because they are bottom of the waiting list. We are human. We can go away and spend the weekend worrying about what might be happening. We need to off-load and to share our unhappiness. We need to take this on board and to find ways of dealing with the work's stressful effects.

Mrs Kennedy rang her social worker at least once a month. She cared for her mother who had dementia, she had a young family and worked part time. Roughly every month Mrs Kennedy would feel that she could not go on any more and would ask the social worker to arrange for permanent residential care for her mother. The social worker always responded and by hook or by crook would have some respite care or a permanent bed arranged within days of the call. At the last minute Mrs Kennedy would call and say that she could not face putting her mother away for good. Sometimes she would use some respite care, sometimes she would not. But the need to make arrangements and plans would be played out again and again.

In this situation the carer needed to know that help was there and that the worker would respond. For the worker it meant frantic activity, getting resource holders to part with services and listening to Mrs Kennedy when she felt at the end of her tether. The social worker needed to deal with feelings of annoyance, find time for this last minute work and deal with the chaos it caused to her diary.

The ways of dealing with such stresses are numerous. Although we might well complain that we never find the time to relax, one excellent way that can be shared with others is to laugh. One busy intake team survived by laughing and singing. On a regular basis they would gather at lunch time and 'do' musicals. Calamity Jane was a favourite that had them reduced to tears of laughter within minutes. Stress needs to be shared. Line managers should be on the lookout for it and workers should not be afraid to hold out a hand to colleagues if they think they may be having problems. A useful description of stressful symptoms is provided in *Social Work Stress and Intervention* by Fineman (1985). For Fineman the key word for stress is threat; workers feel threatened by a perceived lack of competence on their part. They may doubt their ability to judge situations and be worried about going into different arenas where others may see or notice their perceived lack of ability. In such a situation it can be impossible to say that they are having difficulties. It is important therefore that we look out for one another. The dangers of hanging on to worries, and letting these overpower us, will lead to ill-health and potentially dangerous practice.

Another hazard that we may face, or have to deal with, is the aggressive encounter. Being on the receiving end of either physical or verbal aggression is frightening and stressful. It is bound to figure for social workers at some point if only because of the stress and the pressure faced by those with whom we are working. On any stress rating scale, caring scores highly. Families are often under pressure and can be justifiably angry if they cannot secure the help they need. However, whatever the problem and difficulty there is a clear line over which people must not step. Social workers can and should accommodate some of the feelings of anger and frustration that carers or family may feel, but that does not mean we are there to be verbally abused or struck. It may be that in a potentially difficult encounter this needs to be stated up front. We may want to state, at the outset of an interview, that threats will mean that we will leave again. If we feel that we are walking into a highly charged situation then the option should always be open for us to be accompanied. We firmly believe that workers should follow their own initiative in these kinds of situations. If the visit does not feel right, or the situation on visiting is not the one you were led to believe; then leave. Do not worry about trying to make up a reasonable excuse in order to leave without fuss: just go. There is nothing to be lost. In any kind of tussle or situation where someone has to be restrained, then simple rules should be followed. Grab clothing rather than limbs. If holding limbs is necessary this should only at the large joints. Restraint is only ever used when other methods have failed. If you are witness to a physical tussle, you can try to distract those involved with noise. If you have to stop someone from harming themselves, act, and when the situation has calmed, call for assistance. Departments should have in place policies that will outline for staff what they should do in such risky situations.

Never underestimate the shock experienced in such a confrontation. Any incident should be recorded and senior staff made aware of what has happened. A written report of any such events may be needed. Putting a personal version of the event down on paper as soon as possible is always worth the effort.

Of course it is not always easy to predict what might be an aggressive encounter. People who are confused or disorientated may lash out either at a worker or another older person because they feel worried or frightened. Constant swearing may be a usual part of communicating for some and may not be meant as a threat. Someone with aphasia as a result of a stroke, may not understand the purpose of the contact and perceive actions as some kind of threat. Behaviour is often an attempt to communicate. *Screaming and Shouting* by Stokes (1988) is a useful book which addresses aggravating or aggressive behaviour in relation to people with dementia. New workers may find it helpful to discuss threatening or violent behaviour at a team meeting. It is possible to learn a lot from the situations others have had to face. Clues about pitch of voice, actions or movement that are helpful can be shared.

Knowledge

Having thought in some detail about preparing for contact, we need next to consider the body of information and knowledge we should have at our fingertips. We need to know the legislative framework that surrounds our practice inside and out. We also need to understand the benefits and welfare rights system as it applies to older people. We need to understand the physical and mental health difficulties that older people may experience. Some of this can be found in articles and books. A great deal will come from talking with others. It is always worth asking because most people are flattered and delighted to assume a tutor role. Doctors, in our experience, enjoy being asked for information about a particular illness. OTs are usually pleased to talk about the equipment they provide and what makes them consider some people suitable for some aids and equipment and others not.

We need to make it our business to know in some detail about any legislation that can affect an individual's rights, liberty and entitlement to help. Such legislation includes the recent NHS and Community Care Act 1990, the Mental Health Acts, the National Assistance Act 1948, the Chronically Sick and Disabled Persons Act 1970 and the Disabled Persons Act 1986. Copies of acts are held within local offices. We should know where these are, have read them and understand their content. Many departments provide a quick information guide to these. If they do not, it is worth writing one. You may want to dig out and photocopy the relevant sections of the law, to keep for easy reference. Alongside any of these Acts there will be guidelines issued by government and often by departments themselves, that will outline what is to be regarded as good practice in the implementation of the legislation. Such guidelines need to be studied and learned as they will indicate what particular departmental procedures must be applied. Some guidelines are available from HMSO book shops and cover a range of issues from care management, to quality assurance arrangements and good practice for short-term/respite care and discharge from hospital. Your department may have copies but, if not, you might want to think about purchasing copies for yourself.

The piece of legislation with the biggest direct bearing on the social work service provided to older people is the NHS and Community Care Act 1990. Since April 1993 it has placed a duty on social services departments to provide a comprehensive needs assessment to those experiencing difficulties in managing their own care. The Act and accompanying guidelines see the preferred option for the vast majority of older people as having their care needs delivered to them in their own homes, within their communities. The task is therefore for social workers to assess needs, to develop and then deliver packages of care to individuals. A first step is for social services departments to develop policies which can determine who is eligible for assessment and what will be the timescale for assessments to be undertaken. This means describing how quickly the worker will visit once a referral is made and how long the assessment process should take to complete. Once completed, the assessment must be recorded and copies made for the individual and their carer. General guidelines have been provided on the issues and areas in the assessment process. The Department of Health guidelines entitled *Assessment and Care Management for Practitioners* (1991) (there is a separate copy for managers) is useful. Many departments have used the guidelines as reference material to work out their own standardised assessment forms and so ensure that all areas are covered. When an assessment is complete and a care plan or package devised, information about its implementation should be provided to all involved. This includes the individual, family and other service providers. If the older person or carer is not happy with the assessment either because of its process or because they feel their needs have not been identified they can appeal against the plans made. If needs cannot be catered for then this information too is generally recorded by departments, so gaps in service and unmet needs can be identified. Departments are further encouraged to develop channels by which they can involve older people and their carers in planning and influencing services that may be used as part of the package of care.

We need to know in some detail about all the duties and responsibilities that the Act and our departments expect of us. We need to be able to explain the process clearly to the older people and answer queries or questions.

Of the remaining field of welfare legislation, it will be the particular circumstances of an individual that will dictate which Act and what parts may be useful or applicable. The first to think about are the Mental Health Acts as they apply across Britain. There is a percentage, albeit small, of older people who are admitted to hospital each year under compulsory admission powers. They may be admitted for treatment or observation or they may be taken into Guardianship and have their place of residence determined for them. Action under the mental health legislation may be begun by a doctor or a social worker. If a social worker, it will be a specially trained and approved worker who has a body of knowledge and expertise in the mental health field. If we are concerned about the mental state of someone we are working with we should feel able to call upon the Approved Social Worker (ASW) or Mental Health Officer (MHO) in the office for advice. It is well worth finding time to accompany the ASW/MHO on their work for a day or two to discover the situations in which these Acts are likely to apply.

Section 47 of the National Assistance Act 1948 describes a power we need to be aware of and approach with some caution. It is thankfully used only very sparingly and in some local authorities its practice is banned altogether. This piece of legislation allows for the removal from home of any older person who is deemed to be aged, living in insanitary conditions, suffering from grave chronic disease and not receiving proper care and attention. It first saw the light of day in the Bradford Corporation Act 1925 and was introduced in order to facilitate slum clearance. It allows for people to be taken from their homes, with no appeal or redress and to be placed in some form of care for up to three months. In our opinion this is an ageist piece of legislation which lacks clarity and proper safeguards. It should only be used in very rare situations when someone is too physically ill to make a rational decision and where there is a strong likelihood that the admission to care or hospital will ensure their recovery. One of its chief dangers it that it does not require a social worker to be involved. The only players required by law are a magistrate, a GP and a community physician. By and large it should be given a wide berth and should only be a topic of case conference discussion when other methods have been tried and failed.

Other legislation to consider is the Chronically Sick and Disabled Persons Act (1970) and the Disabled Persons Act of 1986. Both acts have something to say about entitlement to service. For example, section two of the Chronically Sick and Disabled Persons Act states that local authorities have a duty to meet the needs of the disabled and chronically sick once these have been assessed, although they do have some leeway to determine the degree of need. Entitlements under this legislation can cover things such as adaptations, telephones and access to educational facilities. Workers should cross-reference these requirements against the new duties under the NHS and Community Care Act to make sure that the best possible advantage is being offered to the people with whom they are working. If your department is only in a position to identify need, but not within current resources to meet the need, it may be that reference to the Chronically Sick and Disabled Persons Act will make the much needed service materialise.

Another kind of legislation altogether is that which relates to the funds and property of the older person. Power of attorney and enduring power of attorney enable someone else to act on the person's behalf. These can only be given when the older person is of sound mind. It is often worth advising an older person to be sure that they have organised an enduring power of attorney in case they are unable to manage their affairs for a long period. If someone is plainly unable to manage their financial affairs and they have significant assets then the Court of Protection (Curator Bonus in Scotland) may be the answer.

Rights and Risks by Alison Norman (1987) covers a good bit of this ground in relation to powers of attorney and Court of Protection. Other useful publications include *The Law and Vulnerable Elderly People* (1986) produced by Age Concern England and *Dementia and the Law* (1988) by Scottish Action on Dementia. Both look at existing arrangements as well as ideas for new legislation.

We may also want to advise older people on how to go about making a will. Often people have a real need to pass something on to their children and grandchildren. Making a will is the best way to do this.

We need to have knowledge of the full range of benefits and additions to which older people are entitled. We need first to understand how the state pension system works. If an individual is not receiving a full basic pension this should be checked with the Benefits Agency. There may, for example, be credits because of Home Responsibilities Protection (HRP) that have not been added, or paid work in another EEC country which has not been notified. Claims for the retirement pension are usually made three months before the retirement date is due. A form will be sent out for the person to check and indicate any omissions etc. Dependent on how much attention such a letter is given, errors may go unnoticed. Particular attention will need to be given to older people who have never registered for work.

It may be for example, that if a person emigrated to Britain but then did not seek work, they may grow into old age without a National Insurance number. This will cause problems when they come to seek any pension or benefits. In such a circumstance they will first need to apply for a number and then pursue a claim for a pension or any other benefits. This can be a long process involving contact with the Home Office as well as the Benefits Agency.

Some old people may have pensions from other sources. This may be as an additional pension or a graduated pension from their place of work. Both pensions are taxable and will certainly affect a person's entitlement to Income Support and Housing Benefit. If someone is paying tax on an additional pension they are very likely to be receiving tax returns, to be completed on an annual basis. Such forms are quite long and difficult to complete, so we may find ourselves helping in this process. If someone is paying tax but is not being asked to complete a tax return, it might be important to think about whether it would be to their advantage to do this. There may be some areas of expenditure that can be claimed against tax, which may have the effect of bringing down that individual's overall taxable allowance. It may only be a very few people who are in this position, but we do need to be aware of it as an area that might need checking.

Entitlement to Income Support must always be checked out. We need to be aware that people on Income Support can claim lump sum Community Care Grants. It is not necessary to wait until a piece of household equipment expires before a grant is made to replace it. We should ask what people are having difficulty with and see if a grant would be appropriate. Mrs Harper had not really thought about replacing her cooker until the social worker suggested it could be a possibility. She had lived for many years with only one of the four top rings working and a functional grill but no oven. She had just got used to eating meals that could be cooked in one pan or having more cold than hot food. A Community Care Grant was applied for and Mrs Harper was able to have a new fully functioning cooker.

The Attendance Allowance is probably the most well known of the benefits older people can obtain. It is a benefit intended to help people with the costs that come with being disabled. Anyone who is having difficulties managing their own self-care, or who needs a degree of supervision, can apply. The Attendance Allowance is paid at two rates dependent on whether a person needs help from another during the day, or during the day and night. The Attendance Allowance forms presently in use come in two parts. A first section asks for basic information about the person wanting to make a claim. The second asks for details on the difficulties being experienced. Towards the end of this section, two statements need to be completed. The first can be completed by the carer, the second by someone who knows about the person's medical condition. If there is not a nurse or doctor who could complete this part quickly and easily, then we may want to think about having a go at this ourselves. It may be that we have learned a great deal about someone's condition from medical personnel or because we have attended case conferences where this has been discussed. We will know from their visits what prescribed medication the person takes. Having this knowledge, it may sometimes be appropriate for us to complete the form. Some social workers have completed this second statement and this has been acceptable to the Benefits Agency.

Attendance Allowance forms can be daunting to complete. Many people need help to express themselves appropriately on such forms. This may mean getting the older person to think about the different circumstances in which they may run into difficulty. For example, some one may be able to walk 20 yards to the shops, but in very cold weather when their chest condition is aggravated, walking less than ten yards may leave them breathless. It is important to bear in mind that receipt of Attendance Allowance may bring additional money, possibly Income Support via the addition of the severe disability premium in the entitlement calculation. It is always useful to have to hand one of the many useful guides on benefits. The annual Age Concern publication *Your Rights* (1995) is excellent. In Scotland, *Dementia and Money Matters: A Guide for Carers* (1990) looks at a range of issues related to people with dementia. This booklet is available from Alzheimer's Scotland Action on Dementia.

It is worth taking some time to work out a personal checklist of benefits to tick off in any particular situation. This list would include benefits that might be available to those suffering with a particular problem such as sensory impairment. It would also cover benefits available outside the realm of the insurance and social security systems. These include rebates on television licences and exemption from some motoring costs. Such a checklist can sit very handily in the front of a diary and also act as a reminder to discuss money issues. Such a checklist should be needs led; for example, list what the benefits are if a person lives alone and what applies if help is needed with personal care. If someone is blind or partially sighted what discounts do you need to check for? If they are in receipt of mobility benefits, what help with motoring costs could be found? A quick way to put such a list together might be to have a quick brain storming session with a welfare rights worker. This information should be at their fingertips and so they will be able to reel off the information you need to know. We need to keep our eye on the Council Tax and the various discounts and exemptions that may apply. The Council Tax can be a mine-field for older people because it has so many component parts.

Teams can divide up their expertise in order to cover all these complex areas, having one worker who knows Council Tax, another national insurance issues and so on. This way workers can provide more detailed information and a source of support for one another. Welfare rights work does take time. It may be that two or three visits are necessary for a worker to convince someone of their entitlement, before then encouraging them to apply. Money is a major issue for older people, particularly with the increasing emphasis on charging for services.

So, although money might feel like a difficult issue to raise, it must be addressed so that older people have the opportunity to maximise their income.

In undertaking this work it is also important to accept and listen to an individual's priority for expenditure. Mr Hastings paid a gardener a precious £7 per week to work three times a week on his medium size garden. The social worker working with him to budget his money and so pay off some of his debts, tried for months to get him to give up this expense. The promise of armies of volunteers who could come and do this job did not move him. Mr Hastings spent hours in his back room watching the garden. For him it was better than the television. Watching the birds coming and going, the next door neighbour's cat trying to catch them and finally watching the seasons change, filled his day. He wanted his garden done well and enjoyed talking to a knowledgeable person about gardening matters. After some patient work the social worker was able to recognise the gardener as a long time carer who did other unpaid jobs for Mr Hastings: things that the worker had been unaware that Mr Hastings was unable to do for himself. An attendance allowance was applied for and used to meet some of the unpaid bills.

A second money issue for social workers is to give advance warning of charging policies where these exist. Many of us feel a certain reluctance in talking about this area of business. It may be that we feel uncomfortable with the fact that people should have to pay for vital help. This hesitancy must be overcome. Older people are fully aware that all sorts of services have their price and most would prefer to know sooner, rather than later, what costs might be involved. Charging for residential care needs to be carefully explained, probably more than once. Time is also needed for the family to discuss such arrangements.

The biggest area of knowledge for us to get to grips with is physical and mental health problems. We need to have the facts about the usual progress of dementia, how it may manifest itself and what might be the impact on the person in terms of them functioning in their home environment. We need to understand what might cause an acute confusional state and the symptoms of depression. If an older person has had a stroke, we need to know the physical and mental implications of this.

We need to know about medication, what dosage is usual and if the older person is aware of the side effects of what they are taking. There is limited space to go into a great deal of detail within these pages. Each of these topics would easily use a book on its own. However we have provided some information in the appendices and have suggested in the reference page further useful reading.

We hope, in this chapter, that we have covered the ground as far as preparation for work with older people is concerned. The next chapter covers assessment.

5

The Assessment Process

Social work with older people is now centrally concerned with the carrying out of assessments. Within the community care framework, assessment is part and parcel of a care management approach. Care management aims to offer a more systematic long-term model for the management of the care of older people, specifically those who wish to continue to live independently in their own homes. Screening, assessment, care planning, implementation and then monitoring and review, are all components of this process. Assessment may be carried out at a number of levels. There might be an assessment for a specific service or one that has a wider needs focus, as in a community care assessment.

The emphasis on achieving a throughput of community care assessments for the large numbers seeking this service, means that we need to be very clear about the meaning of assessment as well as understanding what elements make up this process. Any of us can undertake visits with the aim of achieving a general picture of an individual's living situation, but a proper assessment can only really be undertaken when there is something to be assessed for. This means that there has first to be some kind of identified need or needs that are the focus of the referral. Once a worker is involved with the individual, they may uncover other problems that need to be tackled. As this happens the assessment process will develop to encompass these and so a more complete picture will be achieved.

There is a view, held by some managers, that assessments can be completed with one or two visits and with just the gathering of a basic picture and the introduction of a resource. However, working with older people is not really like this. There are often immediate and urgent problems to be solved. Older people often take a dim view of someone who asks hosts of personal questions and fills in a form, without showing any inclination to address the obvious problems. Many older people live with the realisation that time is not on their side and help is needed speedily. We need to think imaginatively and never lose sight of what it is we can personally offer to change a situation there and then. This may mean offering practical help or thinking of an intermediate solution to a problem until the appropriate resource can be accessed. Mrs Stewart had been promised by the Day Centre Organiser that she would attempt to find her a volunteer to help her settle into her new flat. When the social worker called some weeks later to undertake a community care assessment, Mrs Stewart was a little on guard, because she initially feared that the social worker might see her flat in disarray and conclude from this that she was not coping. Instead the worker got a couple of screwdrivers from her car and gave Mrs Stewart a hand to assemble some of her newly purchased flat pack furniture. This sorted a practical problem for her and encouraged her to feel that the social worker was really there to help her.

Taylor and Devine suggest in their book *Assessing Needs and Planning Care in Social Work* (1993) that there are a number of component areas to the process of assessment. These start with making sense of a situation, building up a picture of what happens and then identifying problems. From this we need to relate the person to the legislation and policies of the department, identify the strengths and weaknesses of the individual to address the problem, identify difficulties and clarify expectations. We can think ourselves through each of these stages as they suggest themselves. They do provide a helpful guide to ensure that the older person is kept central to all the work being undertaken.

We intend in this chapter to focus on the step by step process of undertaking an assessment and to look at some of the areas of involvement that can follow once needs have been identified. This will be very much a blow by blow account of the process and so may cover some beginning issues with which readers are already very familiar. However we make no apologies for revisiting some of these basics, they are important considerations in working with older people and cannot be said often enough. Hopefully for those new to this care group, such a process will assist in the identification of specialist skills and preparation work that are essential to work successfully with old people.

The referral

A starting point for all work is to look at the referral. Referrals come into the office from a variety of different sources and may be patchy in the information they offer. If there is not enough information or it is not clear, we should start by getting in touch with the person who made the referral in order to confirm the reason for the referral. This can be particularly important if the referral has been made some time ago and so needs to be updated. Contacting the referrer will let them know that the referral is now receiving attention and offers an opportunity to confirm that the older person is aware of the referral. In some situations it may be that the person making the referral does not know the older person particularly well. It may have been the doctor's receptionist who phoned through to the office to say that the GP felt that Mrs Smith needed help and that she should be seen by a social worker. The GP may not have had contact since that time and indeed may be not be able to recall, in detail, their concerns. In such a situation we should not assume that the referral is not important or not a priority. It may just be time that has distanced the GP from the referral. If the referrer has no updating information to offer, then we should have a couple of questions to ask in order to fill out the referral. If, for example, the person being referred has chronic health problems, we may want to ask if they have been in hospital in the last twelve months or if they are still being treated as an outpatient. If there have been a couple of admissions in recent times, this may suggest there are more severe problems in coping at home than at first thought. It may also point to additional information being held by a hospital social work team or with the home help service.

In many places referrals are waiting some time before being allocated. One team decided to deal with this by agreeing that when each member of the team was on duty and had a few moments of time to spare, they would attempt to gather additional information in order to complete and update the waiting referrals. Updating the referral information by phoning other people involved can ensure the referral is in the right place in the priority list. Some referrals can actually be dealt with over the phone. We need to remember that not everything has to wait for us. If the referral cannot be allocated for a few weeks, maybe the duty officer can phone and make known the existence of a service that the person could access independently and more immediately. There might be, for example, a home support service offered by a local Alzheimer's group that could make contact straight away, provide a service and offer useful assessment information back to the social work team. Good working relationships with other colleagues can give access to other assessments which enhance our own. If waiting times are very lengthy, phone calls or letters can be made to those awaiting allocation to let them know that they have not been forgotten. Carers may be able to give the dates they need for the respite care. A provisional booking can then be made ahead of the visit so that the opportunity to secure this resource is not missed.

Much of what we are saying here implies that a good referral has been taken. No worker worth their salt will ever just take information. They will ask questions, probe and offer ideas that might help. Ideally this should mean actioning the referral almost immediately, by making one or two calls to get other services and resources involved. The organisation of allocation systems can sometimes mean that the more simple requests end up having to wait the longest. A referral for a day centre placement could be quite a simple matter to arrange. But although simple it will be a low priority where other referrals come bearing requests for assessments for residential care. One team took their duty responsibility very seriously. They had enough people available on duty to deal with referrals, where possible, when they came in. It also meant workers had enough cover to nip out and help someone complete a Council Tax form or make arrangements for respite care, rather than have this wait three or four weeks for formal allocation. Community care teams need to think about how they deal with incoming referrals and have systems flexible enough to respond to a variety of needs.

One team set aside one morning a month to be available to pick up and respond to simple one off requests. In this morning they could go out and attend to telephone applications, reports for charities for information to support an application for a grant and any other bits and pieces.

Right from the start, we can be identifying the useful people to be talking to. A phone call to the district nurses may be worthwhile if they may have had reason to know Mrs Smith previously. District nurses work in people's homes and they are able to pick up a great deal of informal information about how people are managing and who provides the help. They may have noticed, for example, a strain in relationships and may be willing to be involved, working jointly. This kind of information can inform on what approach might be useful and what the sources of concern are for the older person.

Making contact

Having filled out a picture of likely difficulties the next step is to make contact. How this is done should be given careful consideration. Some workers choose to call unannounced. Some may write or phone to arrange to visit. We would suggest for a first visit that workers should write or phone. If a letter is sent it can be read and shown to others. A daughter or friend who has regular contact is likely to be shown the letter. They are therefore informed at the same time that a social worker will be calling. A letter gives time for the older person to think about who is coming and what it is they might want to say to them. They may want to have their house 'ready' and refreshments to hand, as they would to greet any guest. A letter can convey quite a lot of information. It can say who contacted the social services office about the person, information can be offered on what will be talked about and what help might be on offer. The purpose of the community care assessment can be spelt out. Given plenty of notice, the older person can change the date and timing of the visit if it does not suit them or they can arrange to have a friend or carer there when the worker calls. These important choices are lost if the visit is unannounced.

We can, of course, phone to introduce ourselves, but how

well this works may depend on an individual's hearing and on how comfortable they feel about using the phone. If it is suggested from the referral that a particular individual is not keen on strangers calling at her home or that she will not answer the door if she cannot recognise the face, then we may need to work through a third person. In such a situation the referrer will often offer to accompany the worker to make the introductions and help smooth their way. Some workers may be a little wary of this, especially if they feel the referrer may have their own agenda in relation to the individual. However if this is the only way in, then it is an opportunity that should be taken. The skill will be to make sure that the interview is not overshadowed by any particular view the referrer wants to convey and that the focus remains with the individual. It may be very important for the older person to see clearly that the worker is there for them and not merely to reinforce someone else's ideas.

Once a visit is planned, we should turn up on time. Social workers are notoriously late people, but this does not have to be so. Being late is about not planning time well. If we are seen as a busy dashing about person, we may run the risk of being seen as someone without time to listen. Being constantly late is of course just rude and shows little consideration for the person being seen. Old people do have lives and interests, other than waiting for someone to call. No one should assume that old people are a captive audience and that arriving on time does not really matter. There are often good reasons for being late, in which case we should ring or ask someone to. Older people can feel powerless enough without having a sense that visits to them are outside their control. Workers will develop through experience a sense of how long should be spent on a visit. We would say as a rule of thumb anything beyond three quarters of an hour is too long. After this time workers may find that they are going over already covered ground and the older person may be becoming quite tired and unable to concentrate on the issue under discussion.

The first visit

We feel strongly that the first visit is crucially important. It may be the first time an older person has met a social worker. We may seem to be fussing about tiny details but we think they can tip the balance between a visit that is mutually rewarding and one that is not. We therefore take Jane, a social worker through step by step.

Jane has given notice of her visit and having arrived at a person's home, takes time to look at the house. She is asking herself questions from the start. She is looking at the windows, doors and gutters. Do they look cared for? Does it need some repair work? Do rooms look dark, as if they might not be in regular use? As she knocks on the door she makes sure she is standing where her face can be seen. If there is a spy hole, she turns to face it. The person coming to answer the door may want to get a look at her first. If there is not a spy hole she makes a mental note to ask if one is needed. She has her identity card ready. She gives plenty of time for the door to be answered and is not afraid to knock harder if nothing happens. If someone is sitting towards the back of their home they may not hear gentle knocking. She cannot knock loudly with her fists, so she uses the spine of her diary which makes a loud noise (and does not gouge bits out of the door). As the door is opened she steps back so that the older person does not have the feeling that she is on top of them. She greets the individual and offers her name and where she is from. She hands over her ID card and gives time for the person to look at it and at her. She waits to be invited in. This may sound a little laboured but it has its purpose. The person may have been asleep before her knocking woke them. It may take them a few minutes to find their bearings and to know who she is. Alternatively they may have been sitting anxiously waiting to hear the knock at the door and may be flustered now that she has suddenly arrived. She judges each situation as she sees it and takes as much time as she thinks is necessary on the doorstep to explain who she is, the fact that she wrote to them and why she is calling.

Once invited into the house she uses all her senses. Does the house feel cold or just right? Does it smell musty, damp, stale? What sounds can she hear? Is a radio on? Can she hear the hiss of a gas fire? What do the hall and the room she is entering look like? Where is the furniture positioned? Is the hall and room lighting adequate? Taking in this information assists her to get a picture of how an individual is managing and what might be the areas with which they have difficulty. She asks the person to lead the way in to the house so she can follow. This gives her a chance to see how they walk. Does the person use their hands along the walls to steady themselves? Is the person's step hesitant or purposeful? Are they able to stand straight and tall or are they bent with arthritis? Does walking seem to bring discomfort? She takes in this information in order to use it to frame some of her enquiries later on in her interview. On entering a room she always lets the person indicate to her where it is she should sit. They may have a favourite chair they always sit in, or they may have a need to sit in a position near the light so that they can clearly see the face of the person talking to them. How the person seats themselves can tell her a lot about stiffness of limbs or unsuitable furniture.

When Jane and the person are settled, she begins her conversation by introducing herself again and saying why it is she has called. She reminds the person that a friend, their carer or a doctor contacted her and has asked her to call. She explains what has been the person's concern for the individual. If the mention of a carer's or home help's name produces a smile or an acknowledgement then she comes back to this later on.

She often talks about where she works. She explains where her office is and orientates it by pointing out that it is near the Co-op and is the same office the home help comes from. Even if a person forgets her name they may remember she works beside the shops. When she is giving out information, she makes sure she allows space for the older person to interrupt to ask questions or check information. She has a lot of information to convey, but she does not stop listening or giving space for the person to get a word in.

This rather laboured description is based on several understandings. The first is the need to be mindful that for the most part a social work service is being used by people who are in the midst of some kind of crisis. For whatever reason usual coping mechanisms are no longer working. The loss of a carer or a sudden illness may have completely disrupted their lives. The contact that we social workers have with individuals and their families at this time will be when people are at their most vulnerable and open. In this situation the usual defence mechanisms often fall away, revealing people as distressed, unhappy, frightened and angry. This may mean that the older person is unable to offer the information needed or to take in the patient explanation we are attempting to offer. If an older person is not able to articulate their needs, or if they keep forgetting what we are saying to them, it may well signal their anxiety and worry rather than their lack of interest in the interview.

In some situations the older person may have something they wish to say at the very beginning. They may need to unburden themselves of their problems or their worry about the visit. A referrer may have created a particular expectation by making promises about what the social worker will provide. We need to negotiate our way through this and make clear to the older person how their original request fits into the overall assessment process. It may that the older person has requested a particular service and may not be prepared for quizzing on issues they see as having nothing to do with the matter in hand.

There have been some anxieties in the early days of community care assessments that workers have not always explained clearly the purpose of the assessment. Individuals need to know the reason for the visit. If they are unaware that they have been 'assessed' then they cannot disagree with our view and appeal against its outcome. We also need to provide information about the process of assessment and how long this might take. An issue to consider early on may be confidentiality. Older people should know that information identified during the assessment is recorded, and may be shared with others. An older person may be reassured if we say to whom we will be talking about their situation. It may give them some confidence if we say that we will talk to their GP and the district nurse. For them this may be a signal that we are interested and want to do a thorough job. If an older person seems particularly anxious about the visit or the assessment in general, it can help put them at their ease to talk about safe topics like the weather or recent public events. This is a technique we all use socially to give each other time to take stock. Sometimes the first ten minutes of the interview may be about reassuring the person that they are not going to be taken away. Talking about the positives and asking the person what they are able to manage rather than what they cannot, can give them a chance to relax a little and feel comfortable. We always accept a cup of tea if it is offered. In part out of courtesy; but it also provides an opportunity to see the person move, see how they manage making a cup of tea and see how they work within their living space. Accepting this hospitality may be a big issue for the person. They may have prepared something and may have a strong need to be the hostess. Unless they have provided some refreshment they may not be able to relax and take in the content of the conversation. Returning the hospitality by bringing biscuits with you when you next visit may mean a great deal to an older person.

Observation and assessment

Back to Jane and her visit. She is paying attention to how the conversation is developing. Is the older person talking easily and openly? If the person is fairly isolated they may find talking quite difficult. They may need to get used to having a longer than usual conversation. As the conversation proceeds she is remembering what names are mentioned. These could be significant people to talk to later. She is checking out that she has the correct names for family members. Family members may have pet names which are quite different from their given names. She is trying to identify which seems to be the most involved member of the family. Her records may have a son down as the official next of kin, possibly because he is the eldest. However it may be the youngest daughter who has the most contact. If the conversation seems a little fragmented this may be because the older person has some sensory difficulties. If they seem to be straining to see her, she sits forward in the chair, so she does not fade from view. She does not speak too loudly and tries to be distinct. If they are hard of hearing she sometimes uses an amplifying headset and microphone (OTs can have a range of such useful equipment). If an older person is struggling to follow her points, she rephrases the question to see if this helps. When using words like 'assessment', 'respite' and 'home support', she provides some explanation as to what these mean to make them sound friendly and useful. If the older person does not easily converse in English she usually thinks about using a family member or a formal interpreter to help with the assessment. Phrasing and language may need special attention. Elements in our language can convey more than one meaning; we therefore need to be clear in what we say and to check that an individual understands the information we are giving. Mrs Devi came home from hospital without the ointment for her leg ulcer, much to the annoyance of her district nurse. Her explanation was that it stated on the tube 'not to be taken', so she did not bring it with her. This may sound amusing but to Mrs Devi it was not. She had taken literally what was on the prescription and did not understand why she was not getting any treatment. If the person being visited is from a different cultural background, attention may need to be given to the formalities of introduction. Accepting hospitality may again be very important. In some circumstances this may mean sharing a meal or accepting a gift. Refusal may be taken as a dishonour or rudeness and may cause unintentional offence.

In whichever way she is conducting her conversation, Jane has in the back of her mind the gaps in her knowledge that she needs to plug. These may include asking about what contacts the person has throughout the day. What aches and pains they experience? What tablets are taken? What are the worries about money and paying bills?

Open-ended questions help to get the information flowing. This line of questioning is not always intrusive. Often people volunteer this information and will expect to be asked such questions. If someone seems uncomfortable talking about particular issues, then she does not pursue them until she knows the person better. As she talks she is using her eyes. Although she is concentrating on the conversation and giving this her full attention, she is looking at the person to whom she is talking. What is their body language saying that their words are not? Are their hands constantly moving? Are they nervous? Do they have the shakes? Do they seem to have difficulty with making eye contact? How does their dress appear? Do they have the right amount of clothes on for the time of year? Does their clothing appear cared for? Any concerns are then woven into the conversation.

Older people are often pleased to talk about their ailments, as any of us might be when someone shows an interest. Someone may say they have arthritis in their hands. Jane asks what this means. How do they manage to fasten clothes? Can they pick up objects? What pain and discomfort does this give? People often tell her what hurts. If any individual has been struggling with a problem for some time they may have developed ways around it. This does not stop her offering some OT gadgetry that makes life a lot easier. She asks the office OT to lend her their equipment catalogues so that she is aware of the full range of equipment, specialist clothing and household goods that are on offer. There is no need for a specialist worker to come out and identify these kinds of needs. If someone is having difficulty bending to sit in their chair and the social worker sees this, then the chances are that sitting on a toilet is also problematic and a raised toilet seat would help.

Jane asks people how they manage their meals. Is cooking difficult? What kinds of meals are made? Is the older person eating properly? These points are all important considerations and lead into talking about health and medical problems. Probing into someone's medical difficulties does not always have to be intrusive. People often like to talk about their experiences of hospitals and doctors. People do worry about their health problems. They may want to find out what she knows about a particular condition. She is aware that some people may have a different view about illness. In some cultures there may be the view that illness is punishment, which brings shame and means a family does not seek help. She often spends time encouraging people to ask questions and to seek information from the health professionals they meet. She herself often asks her medical and nursing colleagues about the full implications of conditions. People are usually more than willing to share their knowledge and quite often enjoy passing on what they know. We do not expect social workers to become health workers but, in our view, it is important that the most obvious conditions and problems are familiar and able to be recognised.

Jane is able to gather a great deal from just looking at the person. Do their legs look as if they might be bloated? Does the skin look as if it is stretched tight? What is the skin colour? Are there any reddened areas? Are the eyes bright or dull? All of these could add up to something serious waiting to happen. If Jane knows of any existing condition, she knows what a recurrence would look like and is able to judge when it might be important to suggest that someone calls out the doctor.

An important area to be covered in any assessment is to achieve a picture of a person's mental state. As well as looking for signs of dysfunction and mental illness, it also means finding out what makes the person tick. Jane makes observations on the person's mood. Is it cheerful, positive, down or troubled? Is the person able to express their feelings? How much insight do they seem to have about their difficulties? Are they worried or preoccupied? She balances these impressions against what she knows about the individual's personality before the present episode. What coping mechanisms did the person have in place before their illness? Were they usually fairly extrovert or had they always been quite a self-contained person? There may be unspoken concerns about forgetfulness or disrupted sleeping patterns which indicate an underlying depressive illness. The person may have a very real fear that they are losing their mind. They may have heard about dementia and be assuming that their only future is living out their life in a hospital.

A mental health issue may or may not have been indicated in the referral; either way Jane explores it. If the referral carries some reference to a mental health problem, then Jane may go back to the referrer to ask for more information or examples of the person's behaviour. She will be thinking through how to broach this topic with the older person. Communicating with someone who has dementia is not always straightforward. Some people, particularly if English is not their first language, may express their anxiety or depression through the medium of physical problems and difficulties. Expert advice may be needed. CPNs are often the most accessible. We should not be afraid to question what we have been told about someone's mental health. GPs have surprisingly little training about dementia or associated problems. A CPN can provide a more informed opinion. If, for example, people report that the person has become suddenly confused, then it may be an acute confusional state perhaps caused by an infection or stress. Dementia usually has a gradual onset. If some of the behaviour being exhibited is quite unusual Jane may want to think about other possible types of mental illness, for example paraphrenia.

A lack of progress in interviews may be because the older person needs to see us prove ourselves. This may mean undertaking some practical tasks to show that we mean business and that we are keen to try and help. If it looks as if an older person is floundering, finding even the smallest tasks a hurdle they cannot face, then we may need to lift that load. Such action may mean that the person can leave behind one area of worry and can begin to trust and develop a relationship with the social worker. Mrs Casey illustrates the balance of practical and emotional problems in someone who has come to ask for help. Mrs Casey was referred to the local office by her GP who said that she was not coping. Mrs Casey had changed from being a very organised active woman with set routines for her week, to one who forgot to pay bills and had lost interest in shopping and in meeting her friends at the local shopping centre. Mrs Casey was adamant that she did not want a home help and that she could do things for herself. The social worker took time to get to know Mrs Casey. She discovered that her son had died suddenly three months ago in Canada. Mrs Casey had been unable to find the air fare to attend his funeral and was devastated by her overpowering feelings of letting her son down. Much of what had kept her going through her daily routines was her son's fortnightly call. Without him in her routine she felt, for the first time, completely alone. For five weeks the social worker made it her business to call twice a week and bring food with her. Mrs Casey had not asked for food but the worker knew that things would not look up until she started to eat properly. Mrs Casey was slowly encouraged back into her routine and into meeting her friends up at the shopping centre. When they knew of her difficulties they became more than acquaintances, and extended their friendship to involve her in their lives.

A second area of practical work is the 'roll up your sleeves and get on with it' mode which we mentioned earlier. Quite often the assessments that will come the way of social workers are those where relationships are strained and temperatures running high. This may be within families or within the helping agencies if they are feeling particularly vexed by a frustrating set of circumstances. In these kinds of situations we can walk in and be quickly swallowed up by doctors, sheltered housing wardens, home help organisers and a host of others who may tell us how difficult it is to work with a particular family. We need to listen to all sides, but we may also need to tread on people's toes and just sort the situation out. Mrs Carson lived alone most of the time in a ground floor flat. She had severe arthritis in her lower limbs which meant that her mobility was very poor. Her main source of help came from her home help who called four times a week. Her main difficulty was her son. He lived a short distance way, called weekly and talked her into handing over her pension money so that he could buy drink. This meant that Mrs Carson did not have enough money for food or to pay bills. The home help organiser was particularly worried that her home help had nothing to do during her visits and she did not know for how much longer she could justify sending in this worker. When the social worker arrived to do an assessment, the other agencies involved quickly headed her off and put two solutions to her. Tackle the son and get him to stop visiting, or arrange for long term care, so that Mrs Carson could be properly cared for away from her son's clutches. However what the social worker did was something completely unexpected. Amid cries of 'you can't do that' she went back to the office, had a whip-round amongst the staff and bought Mrs Carson £56 worth of shopping, an action that seemed to stun her other colleagues. They had for so long seen the problem as the son and the disruption to their plans that they had ceased to notice that Mrs Carson had not eaten properly for weeks.

Depending on the length of the first interview and on how the person seems to be feeling, Jane will take some time to go back over some of the information given. Some areas, if they seem hazy, may need to be addressed more than once. This helps to get a consistent story. Dependent on pace, there is a time when you need to move on to more personal and private issues. This is likely to raise the issue of confidentiality again. Asking questions of the older person about their feelings, worries and fears requires acute sensitivity. In this regard, we need to think what we give off about ourselves in any interview. Just as we are busy picking up on mood, voice, tone and so on, so might the older person be, with regard to us. What messages are we giving non-verbally? There is the well known cartoon by Whelan of one old woman telling another that her social worker is very interested in gardening. She knows this because the worker always staring out of the window whenever she is talking to her. We need to think about other ways in which we can convey meaning. Touch is one that is not used nearly enough. Messages of support and understanding can be conveyed by touching someone on the arm or holding their hand. If someone is very disabled, words and the effort of talking may become burdensome. Sitting and holding someone's hand while they cry might be all we need to do. Older people may be starved of physical contact and may warm to someone who is not shy of touching them. We will need to judge each situation so that we do not run the risk of invading someone else's space by touching too frequently or continuing if the person seems uncomfortable with this.

Some of the information we seek is of a personal or intimate nature which may cause embarrassment. People often say some quite surprising things. Mrs Rushton told the social worker that her husband had venereal disease during the Second World War. She knew this because her doctor had received a letter from an army doctor suggesting she be examined to see if see might also be infected. She found the examination a terrifying experience and one which made her feel dirty and used. Yet she had never discussed this with her husband. He did not know that she knew about his infection, nor did any of her children. Mrs Rushton had never told a living soul about this. The social worker assured her that it would be held between the two of them and that it would not be recorded in any case notes. Mrs Rushton had waited a long time to tell someone, but that was all she wanted to do. Just once to say it out loud and have someone know how terrible she had felt.

If someone is having difficulty expressing themselves, it may help to offer a chance to talk about past life events. A lot of feelings can be expressed in reminiscence which cannot be talked about in a more straightforward fashion. Tales of times that were particularly frightening or worrying can indicate current fears and preoccupations. We need to be alert to the feelings behind the stories. Why does Mrs Cain have to talk about her children? Is it because, like so many other women, her years as a wife and mother were the most significant to her? Is it because she needs to reassure herself that she was once important to other people, rather than the liability she feels now?

Mr and Mrs McCafferty are both in their 80s. Mrs McCafferty, a severely overweight woman, had become reliant on her husband as she became increasingly housebound. A stroke made feeding difficult. Mr McCafferty, a disabled but alert man, found it increasingly difficult to assist his wife. On discharge from hospital the home help organiser had arranged a home help to transfer Mrs McCafferty to and from the bedroom in the morning and at night time. Mr McCafferty had explained he could manage the meals and feeding Mrs McCafferty. A month after these arrangements had been organised the social worker received a distraught call from the McCafferty's daughter. She had reached the end of her tether and she wished her mother admitted to residential care immediately. She felt she could no longer cope with helping her parents, her husband had been made redundant, her son at college needed financial support and she had to go to work full-time. She stated that she could not continue to go to her parent's house every day to feed her mother.

The daughter's needs, the social worker learned, had not been heard before. The home help organiser had been assured that Mr McCafferty could feed his wife. He had wanted to, but could not cope. His daughter, known to the home help organiser but not spoken to, had been preparing meals for both her parents since the stroke. Mr McCafferty did not think it right to tell the home help of this change in their arrangements. After speaking to the daughter at some length, the social worker sought more home help time, to include meal preparation.

Talking to the families of older people, provided they agree, is often essential. Those people who take on the task of caring for older people can often be assumed to be coping when they cannot. Guilt, sometimes the fear of cost, and ignorance of what help is available can drive people like the daughter of the McCaffertys to desperate and unrealistic solutions.

Family members, neighbours and friends – the unsung body

of carers of older people – are often willing to share the work of caring. Not only do they have needs, they are also important sources of information and, just as important, are potential and actual partners in care. A social worker who ignores carers, when older people have complex needs, helps neither the carers nor older people.

When the views of family carers are being sought, the older person may want to talk about what will be said about them to their family. If an older person knows that their daughter is likely to ask you if you feel mother is safe to continue living alone, the older person may want to hear the response first. We should not be surprised to be asked what we think. The older person and certainly their family will invariably want to know. Such questioning may come as a surprise, but it should not really. Older people see social workers as having some status and a decision making role to play. They expect us to do more than match them up to available help. They will want to know what we think. Mrs Gallagher had been to visit a nursing home with the social worker on two occasions trying to make her mind up about whether she should make it her home. On the second visit, and in front of the officer in charge, Mrs Gallagher asked the social worker what she thought about her going into care. The worker was taken aback by this question and lamely stated that it was up to her. Mrs Gallagher looked saddened by this response and the worker felt that Mrs Gallagher never really trusted her after this episode. She felt that she had let her down just when Mrs Gallagher needed her to be totally honest.

The perceptions we might give to a carer in an assessment need careful thought. It can be quite easy to be drawn into a conversation with one member of a family who may want to know whether we agree with them that other members of the family should be doing more to help out. We need to have thought through how we might respond to this so that we do not unwittingly find ourselves party to a family feud. We cannot assume that families always share the information that we may give to one member. There may be an agenda for one relative to hold on to information and in doing so become the person seen to be in charge. In some situations a worker might see a family in need of some counselling. If this is the case then time must be negotiated for this work to be developed beyond the initial assessment stage or an appropriate referral made.

The assessment process is clearly also about probing and possibly challenging. The information given may well be conflicting. Some of this checking of facts and discussion of emotions will be about more than just getting facts and information right. Everything heard, seen or observed needs to be balanced against the assessment of the situation; as a way of checking information for accuracy. The assessment also needs to be checked against the older person's standard. The assessment process is not about the right and wrong ways to do things. It has to feel comfortable for the older person. If someone only has a bath once a week or fortnightly then this is what should be provided. If someone only changes and washes their external clothing once a month, then this is their standard.

To complete the picture our social worker Jane will need to try and see the older person in a number of different settings, in their day centre or while they are in respite care, for example. This may give a chance for people to be seen coping with different environments and may offer opportunities for more personal and confidential discussions.

Risk

In talking about assessment we have so far concentrated on the more concrete areas of what can be seen, heard and observed. However in compiling the picture we also have to weigh up risk. Most accidents are said to happen in the home. It can be a dangerous place particularly if you are infirm or battling against disability or illness. What were once straightforward domestic tasks may now become difficult and risky undertakings. A person who is unable to acknowledge risky situations or unable to exercise precaution in their actions, for example, by going out in very cold weather without wearing a coat or leaving the gas cooker lit and unattended, will sooner or later raise concern about their welfare. Assessing the difference between the right to self-determination and the lack of ability to see ever present dangers is a clear task for the social worker. An individual may make a choice not to have a home help even though they have recently spent some time in hospital and a home help has been recommended by the doctor. Their need to convince themselves that they are still able to do things for themselves, albeit it more slowly, may be the important issue. It might be that, in time, the person may wish to think about having the suggested home help, but when it is their decision and not the doctor's.

Of course, for some, there may not be any recognition that their action, or lack of it, presents any risk. Some people may not have thought about risks or hazards in quite the way that we can see them. If someone has lived for years with broken furniture it may present a problem for us, but not for the older person. An older person may know just how to negotiate their way through their cluttered home and might be completely lost if furniture is moved and tidied away. If someone is burning out the kettle because they have forgotten they put it on, they will not necessarily be helped by being provided with a new electric kettle, if this is then also put onto the cooker to boil. Risks of course come in small and large varieties. One of our first tasks is to get the scale of risk into perspective. Risks can broadly come in three types: those that might never happen, those that could happen and those that might have to be faced or encountered in any day or in any activity. Brearly's (1982) work on developing personal risk hierarchies goes on to refine these types into a hierarchy of risk which is based on the differences between psychological and safety needs and psychological self-esteem and self-expression needs. When this is done workers can then go on to develop an understanding of how older people themselves rank risk.

A good starting point in reviewing risk is to ask the older person what it is they worry about or fear happening. Some people may have very different concerns from us.

Sometimes we can be too close to a situation to be impartial. Involving another worker can help. An area team social worker asked a colleague from the standby night duty team to call on a lady she was visiting. Mrs Donnellan lived alone. She ate very little, wore layers of the same clothes day and night and seemed to have lost interest in life. Mrs Donnellan always appeared anxious and told the worker that she did not want to be a trouble. The standby social worker was quite shocked by Mrs Donnellan's plight and wondered why the social worker was not working towards residential care with this individual. The standby worker felt Mrs Donnellan was very lonely and frightened about the future and was not surprised when she responded positively to the idea of trying some respite care. The social worker was greatly helped by this assessment. Her anxiety about upsetting or frightening Mrs Donnellan had stopped her from introducing the idea of care. Social work means making assessments and judgements about a wide variety of difficult situations. This is not an easy job. We need to call on all our experiences and knowledge in order to think about what might help. However like any part of life, we can get too close to situations. The social worker's worry about upsetting Mrs Donnellan hindered her from seeing a problem that may have been obvious to everyone else. If we find ourselves locked into such a situation we should not feel embarrassed about using other social work colleagues to recheck our assessments. There is also no harm in asking other professionals for their opinion. Those with an eye for other sorts of problems, such as doctors, nurses and OTs, can see things with a different perspective and often identify solutions outside our remit. This can be seen as good quality assurance.

A useful way of helping anxious professionals discuss risky situations and get feelings and worries off their chest is to call a case conference or case discussion inviting all the interested parties. Some social services departments have mechanisms in place for doing this. But even if they do not exist they can be invented. People may need to get together to recognise that there is nothing to be done. It may be that a plan of action cannot be put together. Methods and options have already been put to the test and failed. The purpose may be, rather, to put everyone in the picture so that responsibility is shared. It may well be appropriate to ask the older person and their family to attend such a meeting so that they can hear and acknowledge the worry that others might have about them.

Charges

Social service authorities have powers to levy charges for social work services; with the limited budgets available to Committees, many authorities now impose charges. Charges can have a profound impact upon the social work task of assessment and helping older people to obtain the support they need.

Mrs Docherty was referred to the Community Care Team by her GP; a widow aged 83, with severe arthritis and angina, she had never before been in contact with a social services department. The social worker telephoned the day of the referral to make an appointment to visit Mrs Docherty. Mrs Docherty wanted to know how the social worker had got her telephone number and said it was not convenient to visit. Pressed by the social worker she eventually agreed to meet a week later. The visit was difficult. Despite evident need Mrs Docherty refused all offers of assistance. As she was leaving the social worker was thanked for her visit and told, 'My sister cannot afford it, nor can I'.

The social worker asked if she could explain about charges, and about benefits. Within the hour Mrs Docherty was willing to accept a visit from the occupational therapist and the home help organiser. She had heard that social workers charged for their visits. She had modest savings and thought that she would have to pay at least £25 a week for help. She had not heard about the attendance allowance or about the sliding scale for charges which happened to be in place within that department.

There are many Mrs Dochertys. Money to pay for help is increasingly an important issue. If there are charges for services these are sometimes difficult to understand. They also sometimes seem to be unfairly applied. They are sometimes seen to be expensive for the service that is provided and so not a rate for the job that the older person may expect.

The social worker's task with the older person and, if appropriate the carer, is to assess needs and to agree ways in which those needs might be best addressed. Services, for example bathing and laundry are now provided, in some areas, by private and voluntary organisations which themselves may levy charges. Private home care agencies are expanding. Some authorities will only organise services provided directly by the authority, but all authorities will support the social worker in providing information to older people about what services are available, and at what cost. Some authorities, where social workers have their own budgets, are willing to buy services directly from independent agencies. Whichever authority we work for we should be well informed about charges and the effect they have on the choices that older people make.

Putting together the care package

Let us rejoin Jane to see how she is faring with her assessment. As she begins to think about the potential care package Jane has a reasonably clear idea about the tasks that need to be addressed with the older person and the time span needed to complete these. She has identified the number of contacts that need to be made, be it with other workers, neighbours, friends or family. She has thought about who needs to be seen or who can be phoned. Family members, carers and other service providers may need as much time, contact and support as the older person themselves. Carers may have a desperate need for someone to hear their story, for example, giving time for them to talk about how a caring role has had an effect on their lives. Jane makes time for this and arranges to see the carer away from the caring situation so they can be encouraged to relax and to talk more openly. Many carers may be unresponsive to some of the suggestions made. This will not be due to lack of interest but more likely to be from the effect of prolonged strain. In a family where there may be a number of carers, time needs to be given to all. Messages do not always get passed on.

In some situations, this kind of listening runs the risk of complicating the assessment work. There might for example be issues about taking sides, if the older person and their carer are bound up in some kind of conflict. In such circumstances it may be appropriate to ask one of the other workers already involved with the family, such as the district nurse or the home support worker, to give the carer support and listening time. In this way the carer will also have their own worker who can be there to help them address their own feelings about their relationships, their caring roles and other features of the relationship.

Having put together a picture, Jane's next step is to think through what actions to propose. As soon as possible she is providing feedback and progress on plans and arrangements. This is done at regular intervals and can be done in bits and pieces. It is not important to wait until everything is in place before a visit or contact is made to explain what is happening. Some information brought to light during the later stages of an assessment may call for a change of plan and this can be accommodated if regular contact is maintained. If the provision of services is central to the care plan, then Jane needs to explain how these work. This may mean a very basic explanation of what home support is, for example. Why does this worker undertake different tasks from the home help? Jane is able to offer information on the other workers who may need to visit in order to provide specialist resources and introduces these people by name. She may also have to explain how others undertake assessments. Where she can, she should provide information on availability and cost. With this knowledge she can pave the way for others and forearm the older person to ask questions of the service. It goes without saying that it is not helpful to use acronyms.

One of the objectives of community care is that the new assessment process is meant to call a halt to the practice of older people being 'over assessed' for services. Community care should mean that individuals are not being visited by numbers of service providers who then ask the same questions. Community care assessment has, in some areas, cut down on the number of multiple assessments a person has had to undergo. Some assessment boundaries are, however, still up for discussion. One way to understand the issues of multiple assessments is for social workers to shadow other colleagues. For the new worker it may be useful to spend some time with the OT and home help organiser, finding out what they look for and what information they need to provide the most appropriate service. Inviting the home help organisers or OTs for a joint visit at the second or third visit can be very helpful. They can explain what they can offer and make their assessment at the same time. If we really give time to develop good working relationships, we should be able to win the confidence of other colleagues and have our assessments accepted from the start. Where other service providers have to go in, it may be possible that they can accept our assessment and use their visit as an introduction and an opportunity to check on the eligibility for a service, rather than conduct a new assessment.

If Jane has asked others to get involved to offer help or services she must take responsibility for the assessment or checking process that this worker then undertakes. She needs to provide clear information to the service provider on the needs of the older person. Jane should also go back to the older person in order to check out their feelings about this contact. Sometimes the news from the service provider is that there is a waiting list. Jane need not be worried or afraid to discuss the fact that waiting lists do exist. It is much better to give people some kind of warning about this possibility so that they can be prepared. If Jane is waiting to hear from someone about the provision of a resource, she finds it helpful to have a note in the diary to that effect so she can chase them up if needs be.

Getting services and resources from others may take some negotiation. Other service providers may wish to convey some view about the appropriateness of the service they are being asked to provide and may feel under a great deal of pressure from the overall demand they are receiving for their services. This may mean patient listening so that others can share their feelings and concerns. In looking at the availability of services, we should aim to treat everyone with the same degree of fairness and consideration, rather than join in any discussion about who deserves help and who does not. From time to time we may be in the position of having to weigh up resources and make some decisions about who, of a number of people, is able to receive the service first. Being faced with such a dilemma gives us a chance to see what our colleagues in the home help service face on a daily basis.

For the majority of situations it will be a mixture of services that are called for to help support an individual. This will mean talking to people and getting them to agree on who does what. Jane makes time to sit down with the older person and their family to make sure that they are happy and clear about arrangements being made. In some situations where, perhaps, there are a number of providers involved, it may be worth getting people together for a quick meeting to make sure that everyone has the total picture and that everyone understands their role. We may find that some service providers have never met. A meeting might be a chance for them to learn about one another and to share information about other individuals or issues. For some of the services Jane finds it necessary to take the older person out so that they can see day care or respite services for themselves. She makes arrangements in advance for this to take place to ensure that a welcome is on hand at the day centre or respite facility being visited. If this is being undertaken she takes advice from the older person on how to help them move about. Having someone half way out of a car seat is not a good time to think about how to complete the manoeuvre. The best position for lifting some-one is a straight back, stomach muscles in, feet apart and bent knees. A number of booklets deal with lifting and handling techniques. The OT in your office will know where to get hold of these.

As Jane comes to the final pulling together stage, she con-siders whether there is a need for longer term social work in-volvement. There may have been issues raised within the assessment and care management that require social work intervention. This should be viewed as any other service. It may require discussions with the line manager. In some authorities the assessment and care management period can be extended so that the worker has time to address a particular medium term issue. If this cannot be done it may have to wait for allocation to another worker. As the package of care is pulled together Jane will need to assist the older person to make some choices about which services they might want to use to meet their needs and to encourage them to have some say about how services are being delivered, for example, in terms of timing and frequency.

How older people make choices is often a reflection of how they have made decisions throughout their lives. Different ex-periences and different settings will influence this process. Older people, like the rest of us, cannot make decisions blind. They may need to sample or experience, in some way, what is on offer to them before they agree to it long-term. From whatever branch of social services we come, we need to acknowledge that we may need to 'sell our wares' to an older person. This does not mean talking someone into something they do not want. It means being prepared to offer the time and encour-agement to let people see that this is a real alternative and one genuinely open to them. Old people need time to think about what is on offer and to have the opportunity to speak to someone else who has used the service. All of this can aid people to reach a better informed decision.

Mr Forrest was very reluctant to think about respite care for his wife. The couple had always managed to care for each other, but with Mrs Forrest's second stroke this was becoming increasingly difficult. Mr Forrest was most ably assisted by being introduced to another couple who attended the same day centre as his wife. The second couple made use of respite care on a regular basis and could confirm that the care on offer was good. This provided some peace of mind for Mr Forrest and he made the decision to use this service. If choice is not offered then our job is to challenge the range of the provision and to influence the development of new resources. This may mean putting pressure on service providers to open themselves up to be flexible and adaptable to individual needs. Planners do not always have to worry about developing a massive range of specialist services. They should encourage generic service providers to think imaginatively about inputs of training and flexible timing to make their services appropriate to as wide a range of needs as possible.

We can usefully test out services to ensure that they are sensitive to the needs of all older people, particularly those who may not have English as a first language or who may need to follow special observances throughout the day. A recent study by Ellis (1993) examining the ways in which older people exercise choice, found that social workers and assessors tended not to outline the possibilities of choice to follow. They did not want to run the risk of disappointing someone or building up false hopes. Unfortunately this tended to have the knock on effect of making people think that they had to put up with a poor service or go without help. This impression can also be given unwittingly when workers set in place services after just one visit. In our enthusiasm to offer something quickly, we can put an individual under pressure to say yes or no to something they have not had a proper chance to think about.

It is understandable that we can be hesitant about offering choices if we are not completely sure if the alternatives are actually available. But in many ways this is not our decision to make. If someone wishes to hold out for a place in a particular home then we must accept that and, if needs be, defend this view to others.

Records

The paperwork that must be completed in order to meet departmental requirements cannot ever be overlooked. Assessment of need usually has to be completed on an assessment form. In our experience it is often not helpful to try and complete the form while gathering the assessment information although the older person may be helped by seeing what the form is like. Departmental procedures will determine the number of hands the assessment forms may have to pass through before approval is given for the provision of some services. This is usually accompanied by financial assessment, so that any charges necessary can be calculated. Since April 1993 many social workers have expressed concern about their responsibility for financial assessments particularly for those going into residential or nursing care. The need for financial assessment has always been there but in some departments this task was carried out by finance sections within departmental headquarters. Anxiety about assessments and the charging for care has always been a high profile issue for older people themselves. We are now clearly involved in this process. Older people will expect to have to talk about money, so we should not be afraid to get on with it. In the new role of assessor-cum-broker, we can begin to try our hand at negotiating for better deals as far as the costs are concerned. If someone is looking for nursing care and the home of choice is charging, say, £320 a week, £40 more than our department might willingly pay, then we have to learn to haggle for a reduction. If the home has vacancies it needs to fill it is often possible to negotiate a price for an individual. Older people and their families may need reassurance about the large amounts of money that care can cost. They may want to know who will pay for their care if they need extra help or if their contribution decreases as they run out of money. We need to be able to provide some answers to these questions.

Reviews

The next stage for Jane to think about is the review and monitoring of the package. When the assessment is compiled, decisions should be made for a timetable to review the care package and to identify who might monitor the package in action. This may be the social worker who has undertaken the original assessment or it may be a key worker, say, the home help organiser who has regular contact with the individual. In some departments there may be a formal review process dictating who should be involved and including a standardised form to be completed. Some teams have also developed a system of having one team member carrying out a review caseload. Of course it does not follow that every care plan is managed by a social worker. Some authorities have sought to leave this with the carer.

The review process is an important one. It is a chance to check the relevance and success of the care plan. The time of reviews, whether every three months or six monthly, will depend on the complexity of the situation. This is best decided by the group of service providers involved in providing the care package. A mechanism for calling an emergency review should operate if any of those involved with the person are worried about what is happening. All changes to arrangements need to be notified to everyone involved. The review process of course needs to be more than a checking process. It is probably the most vital way that we can address quality assurance. A useful guide is *The Busy Person's Guide to Care Management* by Bob Hudson (1993). This guide provides a way to look at quality issues and at the whole issue of care management.

Quality

At a time when departments want to promote choice amongst older people, they will also wish to be concerned about the quality of what is on offer. Most social services departments have in place quality assurance units. Such units have a role with service providers in monitoring the quality of the services on offer to make sure that departments are getting value for money. As a social worker arranging practical services we need to know what we are looking for in a quality service. This can be based on experience or user feedback or spending time in a facility. It is, however, rather too easy to make snap judgements on the basis of a brief visit. As more and more services are registered we can benefit from systematic assessments.

There is no substitute for going with an older person to a day centre. Likewise if you are accompanying someone to see an old people's home, note how staff appear to treat the people who live there. Is privacy respected? Is there a choice about mealtimes and going to bed times? What activities are provided for residents? Are there individual programmes for all the residents? All of these are valid questions to ask. It may be important to ask a privately run residential establishment about any hidden costs for services. The personal allowance each resident receives should be there for luxuries such as a particular brand of bath oil or soap that an older person may prefer. This cash is not meant for basic provision. Check out what 'therapies' are on offer, for example, reminiscence therapy. Is there any extra charge for these?

A mental check list when going into a home should include the issues from *Inspecting for Quality*, published by the Department of Health (1993). How staff deal with privacy, dignity, independence, choice, rights and fulfilment should be at the forefront of the social worker's mind. These can be applied to every area: meals, management of risk, money, health, activities and so on. If you find something you are not happy with the local Quality Assurance unit may want a report outlining concerns. At the end of the day we need to be prepared to make representations to the resource if we are not happy and, if necessary, ask them to meet formally to discuss these. Pfeffer and Coote (1993) have produced a policy paper entitled *Is Quality Good for You*. This guide takes the reader through four approaches to assessing quality and examining how carers and users of services can be involved in looking at quality issues. Of course any look at quality will also make us look at our own practice.

Particular areas of work

The assessment and care management process often highlights issues and tasks that we need to take on. An admission to residential care or nursing care is an area of work with which we will invariably get involved. Uncovering an abusive situation within a family might be another. Working with someone who is dying or planning a successful discharge will be others. All of these will require a range of skills and sensitivity.

Moving into longstay care

Billy

Having to face giving up one's independence to live in care is a major decision for anyone to face. It will herald a stressful time and cause concerns and pressures for all involved. Living at home may have become too difficult to manage and the older person may feel that even the simplest daily tasks are getting beyond their control. At a time when a person may need to think about alternative living arrangements the world may feel very big and frightening, they may struggle to retain control over their lives and their destiny. Taking someone through such a crisis requires a great deal of energy, understanding and stamina. We may find we need to look to colleagues to discuss our own feelings and pressures about this work. Securing residential or nursing care for someone really requires two pieces of work to happen at the same time; first, with the older person and their family and, second, within the appropriate section of the department and with the old people's home. When making arrangements for care a great deal of information needs to be communicated between the residential establishment and the older person. We need to work hard at keeping all parties informed as to what is happening. We must also be prepared to give time for reassurance, extra visits and whatever else might be needed to make things go smoothly. This process is probably best explained by looking at a particular admission.

Jane, our social worker, has been asked to visit Mrs Brent who lives alone in a crumbling terraced house in an inner city. She has been hospitalised three times in the last 18 months with pneumonia, a fractured femur and a slight heart attack.

She is becoming increasingly forgetful and now refuses to spend any money on heating. She has a home help three times a week, a meals on wheels service and a neighbour who calls each day to keep an eye on her. At 89 she has only one of her contemporaries living in the street. She has no family apart from a niece who lives in the next town. Mrs Brent is alone a great deal of the time and does not enjoy this. Her home help has recently been talking to her about residential care and has made a referral to the social worker asking her to visit. Once Jane has built up a relationship, a discussion around the possibility of additional support follows. For a variety of reasons Mrs Brent indicates her preference is for residential care rather than extra community based support. As the discussion of residential care develops the following course of action could emerge:

1. Jane visits Mrs Brent and talks about some of the homes in the locality as well as ones in the town where Mrs Brent's niece lives. Jane is able to describe the homes, knows the names of the officers in charge and may be able to talk of other people from the area who are now living there. Our social worker brings with her a few brochures from these homes and leaves them with Mrs Brent so that she can look at these in her own time. At the same time Jane rings two or three of the homes to mention Mrs Brent to them, saying that she may want in the near future to bring Mrs Brent for a visit.

2. When visiting again Jane asks Mrs Brent if she has had a chance to look at the leaflets and whether she has shown these to her niece. Mrs Brent said that she liked the look of two of the homes and so Jane suggests a visit for afternoon tea.

3. Jane visits both homes, talks to the officer in charge about Mrs Brent and provides a written report on Mrs Brent's present circumstances. She also asks about current vacancies. If the facility is offered, staff from either or both of the homes might undertake a visit to Mrs Brent's own home to provide additional information and to make arrangements for her first visit.

4. A visit is made to each of the homes, refreshments offered

and questions asked. In one of the homes a couple of residents are invited to join Mrs Brent over tea so that they
can talk privately with her about what they feel about the
home and living in care. Mrs Brent meets the senior care
officer who would look after her if she came for the day.

5. When Jane visits again she discusses with Mrs Brent the
   costs of going into care, that there is a trial period and
   that her home would be looked after while she is away.
   Mrs Brent discusses this with her niece and decides to give
   the second of the two homes a try.

6. Jane contacts the home to confirm the vacancy and to make
   arrangements for Mrs Brent to spend a day there. Jane
   speaks to her line manager and begins some of the financial
   paperwork.

7. Jane collects Mrs Brent for her day at the Limes. She makes
   sure that the home help and neighbour are there to wave
   Mrs Brent off. After the day Mrs Brent is given plenty of
   time to make up her mind and offers of other visits are
   made and accepted.

8. Jane speaks again to the home, to see how they felt Mrs
   Brent managed. She makes sure they are clear about Mrs
   Brent's food preferences. She passes on the name of the
   niece and neighbour who want to come and have a look round.

9. Jane checks that Mrs Brent knows that her admission for
   four weeks is on a trial basis, and goes through with her
   the arrangements that will be made for securing her house
   and possessions. Mrs Brent has her niece sew discreet name
   labels into her clothes and makes a list of everything she is
   taking with her. Financial arrangements are finalised. All
   financial care plans are submitted and authorised for
   placement to go ahead.

10. Jane speaks to the officer in charge about the possessions
    Mrs Brent wishes to bring with her. Arrangements are made
    to transport these.

11. A date for departure is set well ahead, giving plenty of
    time for farewell rituals. The Senior care officer pops in to
    see Mrs Brent to make sure that everything is OK. Jane
    takes photographs of Mrs Brent in her house and at her
    door, with her niece and home help. Jane confirms the
    arrangements with the home help organiser and makes sure

that the home help can come along to visit Mrs Brent on the afternoon of her first day.

12. Jane transports Mrs Brent to the Limes where the senior care officer greets her with tea (or sherry). Another resident looks after Mrs Brent and goes with her to her room to help her and the care worker unpack her belongings. Jane makes sure that any ongoing support such as day care is in place. She explains about the review process that will take place at the end of a four week trial period. Visiting arrangements are checked so everyone knows when they can call.

13. Jane visits at least weekly to see Mrs Brent and to pick up on any issues about her care. She makes sure that Mrs Brent has her phone number and explains that she can make contact with her at any time.

14. After four weeks a meeting is held with Jane, Mrs Brent, her niece and the staff of the Limes. Mrs Brent agrees to stay and plans are made for her to sign over her tenancy and clear her home. Mrs Brent is given the opportunity to go home to collect personal papers and supervise the clearing.

15. A final but important point; Jane contacts the carers to find out how they are doing. How are the niece, neighbour and home help feeling? She may need to offer reassurances. Mrs Brent's niece in particular may want to talk about her feelings and her now different role in relation to her aunt's care.

The reality can of course be all too different. An individual may not accept the fact that they cannot care for themselves. There may be some work to take on in terms of meeting with staff from the old people's home in order to secure arrangements to meet the older person's particular needs. Some crisis situations such as ill-health or the loss of a carer may mean a rushed admission. In such a crisis, a person can end up being moved more than once, possibly through a number of short-term beds until a long-term resource is secured. With this kind of crisis we need to make ourselves freely available to the person with whom we are working. We may be the only constancy in that person's life. We need to give time to support the individual and to explain each of the changes that come along.

In some situations of course it may be the social worker who takes the initiative and suggests that residential or nursing care may be the option because they can see an older person losing the fight to keep themselves going. For Miss Temple it was important to 'blame' the social worker for the fact that she moved into a residential home. Miss Temple was very arthritic and recently registered blind. She had lived alone all her life in a small house that had seen very little repair or refurbishment. She used a coal fire, a dangerous task for her to manage, and an activity that left her covered in several layers of coal dust. Miss Temple would not wait for the home help to assist her but got up every day to have her grate cleaned and her fire set by 7.00 am. As one might imagine Miss Temple fell many times while tending her fire. She was taken to the local Accident and Emergency department, kept a couple of hours, washed and sent home again. Her pattern was becoming such that she was in Accident and Emergency every other weekend. The social worker who had known Miss Temple for over two years saw her being drained and worn away by her struggle to keep going. Miss Temple had refused to look at the possibilities of alternative heating or at a different pattern of home support, indeed the worker felt that changes to Miss Temple's home environment would put an even greater strain on her coping skills. The social worker therefore encouraged Miss Temple to move to residential care. The social worker knew that faced with the question 'Do you want to live in an old people's home?' Miss Temple would never say yes. It would cause her too much loss of face to admit that she was not coping. The social worker began by suggesting a period of respite care. She made the necessary arrangements, booking a placement prior to selling the idea to Miss Temple. Miss Temple agreed to spend a weekend in the home and then agreed to stay over a period of bad weather. This period extended and extended until Miss Temple felt her home was in too poor a state of repair to return. Once in the home, Miss Temple told everyone that she liked it and enjoyed being waited on hand and foot. But she never said that to the social worker. It was important for her to 'blame' the worker and so feel that it was not she who had given up.

In recent times social workers have had an increasing role in the placement of older people in nursing home care. This new area of work may raise issues for workers in how they feel about dealing with the private business sector. This may be something with which we each have to grapple. However, what we should not lose sight of is that it offers to us, and those with whom we work, a new range of services that can be closely tailored to an individual's needs. As well as a new variety of service providers it may also throw up some new users of our services. The NHS and Community Care Act reforms now require a social worker to become involved with a population of people who were not previously social work service users. Older people with severe disabilities had, prior to 1993, been candidates for long-term hospital care. For carers seeing the level of care, attention and supervision their relatives needed, they were often reassured to know that hospital care would be provided. Now many of these people are being told that their parent or partner can be cared for in a nursing home. They may not agree with this view and may not be ready for a social worker to visit them to explore this alternative. Some older people may feel that the involvement of a social worker is not of their choosing and that they and their families would prefer to make their own arrangements. If this seems to be the feeling, we need to act with a fair degree of tact and diplomacy in order to accomplish our tasks. In looking at nursing care as an option over residential care, we need to be able to define our sense of authority and knowledge. What influences us to think about one kind of care in preference to the other? Is the lead taken from other workers such as doctors and nurses or is it an area of assessment in the hands of the social worker? How will doctors feel if they recommend nursing home care and social workers persist with trial periods at home because the department's ethos is that institutional care is only applicable as an absolute last resort? Departments may well have a view on this, given that nursing care will be the more expensive option. Much of this area of work holds the potential for numerous clashes and disagreements between workers of different disciplines. Teams would do well to give some time to looking at the issues and maybe involving residential and nursing home staff in this process. An excellent guide produced by June Neill entitled *Assessing Elderly People for Residential Care* (1989) provides a number of checklists for workers assessing someone and then preparing them for the move to residential care. Many of the issues explored here will transfer, in respect of looking at nursing home care for older people. It is a useful addition to any reading list.

Abuse

Sadly not everyone involved with an older person is both caring and supportive. In recent times the abuse of older people has received wider recognition. Older people can be abused in their own homes, at the hands of someone they know or in residential and day care settings at the hands of trusted members of staff. Because there can often be confusion as to what actually constitutes abuse, many have felt it has gone unobserved and unchallenged. Abuse can be categorised as any mental, physical or verbal contact that is unwanted and results in distress or harm. It can be a difficult issue for workers to see as it will be hidden. It may also be something we do not wish to contemplate. We may be unsure of what our role should be and how we might best intervene.

As a first step we need to acknowledge that abuse happens. We need to see how hard it might be for the person to talk about abuse. Those who have been abused often carry feelings about responsibility and feel that, in some way, they must have brought this on themselves. We need, in all our relationships with older people, to create an openness that will give an older person room to talk about such a difficult topic. We need to introduce the topic if we suspect that abuse is taking place. We must encourage the older person to feel they will be understood and listened to. The older person may want to share this problem but they may not want any action to be taken. We may have to live with this and try to offer support in whatever way we can. Mr Baldwin had lived alone his entire life until his grand niece and her family moved in to look after him. Mr Baldwin had had a slight stroke but was managing very well. His grand niece moved in on a temporary basis as she had been made homeless, but after a couple of months decided to stay on to look after her uncle. She sent him out to a day care centre five days a week, Mr Baldwin enjoyed the centre but in moments with the staff would confide that he would prefer to

come only two or three days a week as he found th[...]
and quite tiring. However he did not want staff to bro[...]
with his niece as he felt she did not really want him und[...]
feet. Mr Baldwin had also agreed to this niece becoming
joint tenant on his rent book and so was worried that if he
upset her she might try and put him out. Mr Baldwin needed
the support of the staff to help him through this situation. He
knew he had done the 'wrong' thing in letting her stay in his
house. But at the same time he felt heartily sorry that she was
on her own with three children and with nowhere to live. Mr
Baldwin did not wish action or fuss from those concerned; he
wanted someone to talk to when the situation became stressful.

We may need to look to the policy documents of our departments. We may also want to think about action we can
take on our own or as a team to bring this topic out in the
open, so that older people can know that there is someone
they can go to if they experience abuse. Maybe a leaflet or an
article in a local free newspaper will reach someone or raise
awareness about the issue. A number of books have now been
written exploring this issue in some detail. Pritchard's book,
The Abuse of Elderly People (1992), is particularly useful in providing
exercises and scenarios for workers to think through their
interviews with older people, families and agencies. These provide
advice on identification, action and prevention. *Community Care*
magazine ran a series of useful articles in mid-1993 entitled
'Elder Abuse: Breaking the Silence'. These articles raised many
useful issues and encouraged many social services departments
to look seriously at their own procedures and policies.

Death and loss

Another area of work that we will inevitably find ourselves working with is death and loss. Working with old people means
working with those coming to the end of their lives. It also
means having contact with carers who are losing the role that
has filled a large part of their lives. We need to prepare ourselves
to face these difficult situations. Working with loss can be very
hard, stressful work. Many of us will not have experienced the
bereavement of a close family member or friend. Some of us

funeral or seen a dead body. Many
are protected from death. They may
he funerals of grandparents or other
y be a topic that has never been
red because it is unknown. Whatever
around, we need to face them. We
lp others face these feelings, so we
our own reactions to the shock of
are likely to face multiple losses as
they get older. Loss of loved ones, loss of health and remembrance of better times can all conspire to leave a person feeling depressed and lonely. When we pick up a referral that indicates someone is lonely and needs day care, the first thing we need to ask is, why is this person lonely? Is this an issue about lack of social contact, or is there something missing from that person's life? If the answer is the second of these, then a place in a day care centre will not be enough on its own. We may need to give time to the older person to talk and cry about their losses. They may not have had this opportunity before. They may not have been allowed to cry by others who were not able to deal with their pain. Some family members may have frowned on such shows of emotion. Worse still, older people may never have been asked how they feel. Reactions to death and funeral rituals will vary between different cultures. Attention and respect must be given to these differences. We should make it our business to become aware of what are important observances, and then go on to make sure all others involved are also aware.

Because a great many people find themselves distanced from death, they do not know how to behave when they are faced with it. We may find ourselves not knowing what to say; whether we should ask the person about the particular circumstances of the death, or what help we should offer. The truth is that there are no right answers to any of these questions. What is vitally important, however, is that we say something. A person's loss must not be ignored. If we cannot find words it may be better to hold their hand or express our feeling for them in some other way. All of this is a very difficult experience to come to grips with if we have yet to confront the reality of death. However sometimes we can use the resources that are around us. We can perhaps talk to our parents about their losses. What emotions and feelings did our mother experience when her father died? How does she describe grief? There can be a lot to learn from these important conversations.

An older person may want to talk about their own fear of dying and of dying alone. A lot of older people worry that they will die and that they will not be found for days. This may be behind their anxiety to have someone call every day. They do not need a home help. They just want someone to check that they are alive. A great many old people think or worry about death and dying. They may not express this openly. This may be a question we, as social workers, need to have the courage to ask. The social worker visiting Mrs Dunn saw little that she could do for her. Mrs Dunn had a heart condition, but she was still able to look after herself in every respect. She still drove her car, which enabled her to get out to the shops and to visit friends. Scratching her head, the worker asked what it was that she could do for her. Mrs Dunn replied that she had no family left and no next of kin to bury her. She was frightened that she would have a pauper's burial arranged by the council. The social worker took Mrs Dunn firmly by the hand and promised that she would take on the arrangements whenever this time came. Mrs Dunn and the social worker arranged a financial funeral plan, that allowed Mrs Dunn to pay for her funeral ahead of her death. A note to this effect was written into the case notes and the GP and consultant made aware of the arrangements. When she died some eight months later the social worker was informed by the GP and the plan swung into action.

Grief and loss triggers a great many emotions. Some may not be to do with the loss being faced, but events that passed long ago. This can also happen for us. Arranging someone's funeral may make a social worker think about the loss of a parent or friend. If this gets too difficult to deal with it may be necessary to say something to the line manager or ask a colleague to help with the arrangements. There are bound to be issues in social work that open up a personal crisis for any of us. We should not be afraid to ask colleagues and friends to help.

Carers who are experiencing loss, may experience many mixed and conflicting emotions. Guilt, loneliness, loss of role, and relief may all hit at the same time, often when there is little free time in which to grieve. Worries about money or finding a job may need attention. The carer may feel completely on their own. All the people who used to visit have gone away. The home help, district nurse and the doctor have all stopped calling. It is important for the social worker to remember to give some time to the carer, before the case is closed and new work taken on. Carole Smith's book *Social Work with the Dying and Bereaved* (1982) and *Loss and Change* by Peter Marris (1974) are both good reads in this area.

Discharge from hospital

Hospital-based social workers will of course have a major role to play in planning discharges. As workers we can think through the considerations that need to be addressed in securing extra resources. However, we need also to be sensitive in thinking through the emotions and feelings the older person may experience as a result of being in hospital.

Discharge from hospital can mean very mixed feelings for the person coming home. They may have a desperate desire to get back to their own homes and their own things, but also be able to acknowledge that they miss the activity of a lively ward. When in hospital you are placed directly in someone else's care. Many decisions and freedoms are taken away from you and this can be very hard to bear. However this is often compensated for by the fact you find yourself protected and cared for by people with a genuine interest in your welfare. If you are stuck in bed, you have no choice but to rely on strangers to do intimate things for you. Having to ask a stranger to help you to the toilet, or to wipe your bum, cannot help but form a bond of some description. For those older people who have lived on their own for some while this may be the first real experience of being looked after they have had for a long time. They will feel close to those who are touching them. For the first few days on a ward people will be settling in and a battery of people come to see them to run tests and take blood. We may want to take as early an opportunity as possible to make ourselves known. A number of hospital-based teams have worked out arrangements within their wards to ensure that an admission notification is provided to the department so that they can be involved at an early stage in planning for care. Workers can introduce themselves to the older person and act, where needed, as an interpreter of what other colleagues and workers are doing for them.

Other teams have also responded to the need for better information on the part of the older person by producing a 'going home folder'. Such a folder includes information on the medical condition for which they have been treated, information about side effects, if this is appropriate, details about the services that can be offered by other hospital staff, who will be seeing them during their stay and finally the all important arrangements for discharge and after care. Making arrangements for people going home means first looking in some detail at how they get there. Waiting for an ambulance to take you home can be a very exhausting experience. An older person may find themselves sitting waiting in a corridor for a number of hours. There may be no one to meet them at home or to get their home ready, by airing the bed, getting in food and putting the heating on. There are implications where someone is going home disabled, in a different physical state from when they left their home. What panic might they feel when they see that their comfortable home of 30 years now seems awkward and wrong. Suggesting to Mrs Wright that she bring her bed downstairs, because she could no longer manage the narrow, steep stairs up to her bedroom, had the effect of sounding some death knell for her. She knew in her mind that she would not last long if the bed was brought down and she was right. If the existing home is not going to fit a person's needs without quite a lot of changes, then it might be appropriate to suggest making a completely new start. Decorating and even one or two additions of new furniture may make a new home in familiar surroundings easier to return to.

If there are likely to be major problems a home visit should always be made before the final discharge so that workers can identify difficulties that may need to be addressed. A recent publication on discharge from hospital is the Neill and Williams's *Leaving Hospital – Elderly People and their Discharge from Hospital* (1992). This raises a number of useful points which identify what hassles we as workers learn to live with, but highlight the major source of anxiety they can be for people caught up in the process.

6
Working with Others

A great deal of social work time is spent in close contact with other workers. These colleagues come from a range of disciplines and bring with them very different ways of working. Although all working for the good of the older person, some colleagues may have very different structures to negotiate to achieve some of the same aims. Given that we can do little to change or influence these other structures, we need to find the most meaningful way of working around them or with them. We will achieve this by getting a grasp of the structures that others work within and by gaining an understanding of the pressures that others may face. Social services departments are the lead agencies in undertaking community care assessments. This is a very weighty responsibility for us and provides a great deal to live up to. However it does not follow that because we have the lead role, we have all the answers. There may be voluntary sector workers or nursing staff who have a whole working lifetime of experience with old people. We can benefit greatly if we tap into this knowledge and sometimes defer to what others know. This means encouraging others to share in the decision making process and listening to what they have to say.

Some of us may already have experienced some animosity from health and voluntary sector colleagues, who seem to doubt our breadth of experience and expertise in the field of community care. If we are honest, then we must admit that they could have some reason for thinking this. Social services departments have not always been renowned for offering a quality service to older people. We may be seen as not having the skill base in terms of specific training and expertise that colleagues can show. However this difference in perception needs to be tackled. What will make the most impression on colleagues with this kind of scepticism is to show them that we are prepared to develop the necessary skills and that we are interested in learning what they know. We can also often forget to be kind. Other professionals may feel very threatened by social workers in their new guise as community care assessors. Health visitors may feel that, for many years, care management was their role with older people. They may feel community care has hijacked their expertise and that their role now is, in some way, being eroded. We need to see and acknowledge this. Giving people a chance to talk about their worries in this respect is a good step in building good relationships. A starting point for understanding other perspectives is to look at the pressures other workers experience. One team went some way to addressing this by opening up its regular monthly meetings with a consultant psychiatrist to local district nurses and health visitors. In the normal course of their work such nursing colleagues had very little direct access or contact with hospital based consultants. They relished the chance to be included and to have an opportunity to comment on people they knew out in the community.

The social services team

The people we work most closely with are our social services colleagues, yet sometimes to older people it seems as if we come from very different organisations. Having a good relationship with colleagues in the home help service and with occupational therapists is the essence of good team working. We may be in different buildings, or organised around different care groups, or with different line managers. For older people these differences can have a major impact on the kind and quality of service received. We as social workers need to do everything we can to make sure the older person has a co-ordinated service.

The home help service (sometimes known as home care service) has changed and has continued to change in recent years. Some of the important changes include: providing help with personal care, including assistance with bathing and incontinence;

providing help at different times of the day and night; providing help seven days a week, including weekends; setting up of task forces for lighting fires or shopping and co-ordinating community alarms.

Whatever the changes locally, we as social workers, need to know exactly what can be provided by the home help service. Good links with the organisers can bring flexible responses to particular needs. Links with individual home helps, with complex tasks, can help the older person and social workers keep a rapidly changing situation under review.

Occupational therapists, in most social work teams, receive well over 25 per cent of all referrals, most of whom are older people. Social workers and occupational therapists will have much to contribute to one another, each being concerned to help the older person maintain their independence as far as possible. Each can contribute, in partnership, towards that goal. The advice of an OT may provide a practical alternative to increased home help assistance, through the provision of equipment of which the social worker is unaware, or an adaptation to living space which may enable older people to continue to live in their homes. An occupational therapist may enhance the recovery of skills lost through a stroke. Joint assessments, referrals to OTs and keeping close to each other is the name of the game.

The health team

We often have contact with colleagues who work to quite different rules and restrictions. Our colleagues in health agencies may be spread along all rungs of the hierarchical ladder. This may mean that there are particular hurdles to be negotiated in order to get access to them. Those nearest on the ground to us are district nurses, practice nurses, health visitors, CPNs and GPs. It is always worth making face to face contact and asking them what they see to be the issues in a particular situation, what they think of the proposed course of action, and whether they will help to get it off the ground. A great many health workers, GPs for example, complain that they make a referral to social workers, and then they never hear what is happening. One of the best ways of providing interagency collaboration is to let the referrer know what is happening. Sometimes something like a place in a day care centre or residential home can take a long time to access. It is still worth keeping others abreast of where things are up to. They may in turn be able to bring some pressure to bear to help resolve the situation. One team of social workers had standard letters at their disposal to send to GPs in order to update them on their contact with older people. The standard letter sent every six months made reference to the services the older person was receiving as well as what plans or arrangements might be in the pipeline. Once the older person's consent had been obtained for this sharing of information, this service was used for all older people in contact with the team. This meant that GPs were kept up to date with people they had referred, and given information about other patients who were also known to the team but whom the GP had not referred. This service to the GPs helped them to keep their own records updated and made sure that they were not missed out from the usual circuit of information. Such co-operation had the effect of making GPs more willing to share information in return and to provide support information for Attendance Allowance claims, medical reports for respite care and so on, where these were required. As a result workers also felt that GPs were much more open and willing to make referrals to consultants at the request of the social workers, as they had confidence in the social worker's knowledge and abilities. Central to this sharing of information was the permission of the older person involved. This was sought at the beginning of the work and checked on from time to time as the need for new contacts developed.

GPs can sometimes be very protective towards their patients. They may not like to think that others are involved without their knowledge or say so. They may be worried that the older person is vulnerable and so feel some need to check out the social worker on the person's behalf. Although this may drive us crazy, it is important to understand why GPs might feel like this. They may have been involved with the same patient for over 20 years, our involvement may only be months' old. They may feel a loyalty and wish to make sure that all those involved with their patient are pulling and working together.

Some GPs are now working within fund-holding practices. This may mean that they are able to do more shopping
around in respect of securing medical services for their patients.
There may be issues for GPs on the expense of some treat-
ments. This is very difficult for social workers to know about
and monitor. It may be worth trying to talk to the doctor about
this. Ideally we may also need to be passing on information
about after care arrangements that will affect some of the services the GP may choose to use. For example, if the GP uses a
hospital outside the local authority's catchment area, they may
need to know that there may be delays in arranging after care
services.

District nurses provide a most undervalued service in the community. Too many social workers fall into the trap of thinking
that district nurses do only nursing work, such as changing
dressings and giving injections. District nurses do a great deal
more. Because they provide very physical, intimate care for
people, they often have a closer relationship than others can
achieve. This means that older people open up and talk to
them more. It may have been the nurse who has been the
only person going in for years, before the social worker and
the home help arrived on the scene. They may brings bits of
shopping when they can, and do other tasks for older people.
They will spend a few minutes to talk to carers, to discuss with
them how they are managing. They will be feeding back
information to GPs to let them know how their patients are
doing. Nurses can have a great deal of information that is useful
to social workers. If we are worried about the health of a
particular individual, we may be able to ask the nurse to do an
assessment visit. They may be able to put some pressure on
the GP to make a referral, or start a course of new treatment.
Nurses can be under great pressure. They do not have the
protection that allocation systems can sometimes afford.
Everything referred to them has to be seen immediately. They
may have eight people to see one day and possibly twelve the
next. It may only be each morning that they know who they
will be visiting. Managing all of this takes a great deal of skill
and resilience. Practice nurses where they are based are able
to take on some minor procedures that may have previously
required a doctor's attention. Because they have more time,

they are in a useful position to talk in more depth with the older people they treat.

As well as having growing numbers of GPs in fund-holding practices, most community and specialist services are now with health trusts. It is early days to know whether this will cause more difficulties in securing resources or not. There is no reason to think that it should. However, it may have some effect in the future on social service provision. One London Borough now has its community mental health services provided by the local trust, following a successful bid by that trust to contract for the work. This may be a pattern to be seen increasingly over the next few years. This may have the effect of changing social care into nursing care. It may mean that people running social services have different concerns. Workers from both camps will need to strive for an understanding of each other's pressures and ways of seeing the world.

CPNs are an important group of people for us to link to. CPNs can work either as part of a particular community mental health team focusing on the needs of the over 65s, or as a more general team attached to particular consultants. As such, some may still be based in hospitals rather than in the preferred community teams. Either way they are often able to link directly into hospital based services which social workers may be interested in accessing. Different areas will have different arrangements for referral to the CPN's services. For the most part nurses will respond to requests to visit that are made directly to them. They may not be able to offer long-term involvement, without the proper referral through the GP to consultant and then to them, but they will almost always go out and take a look.

A frequent problem is the GP who does not want to refer a patient to a specialist service. One way to tackle such a situation may be to ask the CPN to take a look. They can then talk to the GP and the consultant and may coax a referral out of the GP. CPNs can also often provided an additional cover service. The CPN may call at the weekend to see how the person functions when none of the usual help and support services are around. This may be an easier time for carers to talk. A visit at the weekend may help to complete the assessment picture, by having the older person seen at different times and in different situations.

Knowing what pressures other colleagues are under should

help us to find the best way to go about making an approach to them. Health colleagues are constantly assessing older people. They are either looking for new difficulties or looking out for a recurrence of old problems. What they know about assessment they are usually very willing to pass on. Part of the induction for a new worker could be to spend time going out on visits with nurses in order to develop some idea of what it is they look for. This also provides an opportunity to ask about problems or to talk generally or specifically about what would help them in contacting the office to make referrals. One team did this and heard a group of district nurses explain that they did not understand why social workers needed so much information. Why was it that they could not just accept a name and address and a problem and go along and visit? The nurses did not know about allocation systems or the pressures social workers were under. Talking to one another helps to clear the air. We will not always agree, but we can learn where one another stands.

Sometimes we may need to work through our colleagues. It may be the nurse or doctor who has a long standing relationship with the older person. You may come across some older people who constantly refer back to the trusted worker, with phrases like: 'I will do whatever the doctor thinks'. In such a situation it can be useful to sit down with the doctor and the older person to have a discussion about what the issues are. This way highlights the problem for the other worker and gets them to encourage the older person to think about their needs.

For Mrs Jacobs it was important to ask her GP, who had known her for over 20 years, to become involved in promoting the idea of respite care. The GP was the person the family knew best and whose opinions they respected. The GP was only too happy to help with such a request and indeed offered to accompany Mrs Jacobs on her admission to the old people's home.

There are others who social workers also need to get to know but these may be a little further away. Any worker involved with old people will be having intermittent contacts with consultant geriatricians and psychiatrists. These are useful people for us to get to know. If someone has been referred to a consultant, it may be worthwhile sending a letter detailing our involvement and our concerns. This will help them to get a fuller picture and means, often, that they send a letter back, by return. The referral system to consultants is via the GP. However, if the consultant has already been involved either to do a domiciliary visit, or has brought someone up to the day hospital for an assessment, they may regard their door as already open for further work. This means that we can then approach consultants directly to let them know about the changing picture concerning the person they saw two months ago.

Having this open door means that it will be much easier for us to access direct help from the consultant. Consultants working with old people are on the whole interested and dedicated. They have to be. They are working in an unfashionable specialism many of their medical colleagues have little time for. If they have come to work with old people it will be because they too feel this is important work. Because of this, they are very likely to be on our side. Some consultants would be happy to see an open referral system. Their interest is in getting a service out to older people and they will be glad to meet any social workers keen to work with them on achieving this. In order to build good working relationships it may be useful to ask the local old age psychiatrist or geriatrician to come to occasional team meetings or special interest group meetings. They will get to know other names and faces in the team and workers will be able to hear more about the organisation and demands of the hospital based services.

We can make good use of a copy of the Patients Charter. A number of surgeries and health centres are now producing their own guide as to how they intend to deliver their services. It may be helpful for us to know the promised time scales for the delivery of these services. We can then pass on this information to the older people with whom we have contact and check out with them that they are not losing out in any way. Such a charter or statement may also carry information about what might be the charges for any services. Again this will be useful for older people to know.

The voluntary and private sector

As well as health colleagues, social workers are now working with an increasing volume of voluntary sector workers and volunteers. We need to look to their expertise and understand the pressures they must face. Voluntary sector services, where these exist, often operate on a shoestring. They have very useful but scarce resources. When a new project sets up in an area, we often think 'yippee' and start to flood it with referrals for which we have been struggling to find solutions for some time. Some of these referrals may be appropriate, others may be long shots that we hope the service will take on because no one else can help. However, just because services strive to be flexible, it does not mean that they can then be bent out of shape. The organisation may want to know for how long we will use the service. We may not have thought about this and assumed that once in, it is in for life. If we are asking for two slots of home support each week, will we be assuming that the service can grow to accommodate and deliver home support four times a week if the situation needs this? This is not to be negative and put people off using voluntary sector services. It is rather to register that some of these issues are vital for organisations who need to be forewarned about how their budgets might be stretched to meet these kinds of needs. Agencies may also want to know about the plan for the individual and to be given their place in influencing other areas of the care plan. Traditionally voluntary sector service providers have been annually grant aided or funded for fixed periods, for example, Urban Aid funding. It may be that some smaller organisations will want assurances that they will be offered a continued link, once a referral is made. Mrs O'Neill had been referred by her social worker to a local Age Concern Good Neighbour Scheme. The organiser had agreed to put in a shopping service, but saw their role as offering purely a practical service meeting this particular need and not one of monitoring Mrs O'Neill's more confusing financial arrangements. The social worker had assumed that in dealing with shopping, the Good Neighbour Scheme would also pay her bills, collect her pension and attend to other similar affairs. When the organiser sought to make contact with the worker she found the case closed and felt herself placed in the position of having to opt out of something which she had never agreed to.

It may be important to organisations to have some way back, possibly through a care management or review system to get early response to such problems. Some groups, although they offer home support, can also provide small scale welfare rights work or information services. However, some may not have the expertise to do this. They will want to know that should these issues be uncovered they can refer and have these dealt with quickly. Increasingly as we begin to operate with devolved budgets with which to secure services, we will need to work closely with service providers to agree any changes in service delivery as these will have resource implications. This may mean facing the thorny question of asking service providers to compete, in order to secure the best financial deal.

Social workers vary in their experience of the voluntary sector, these Experiences may be mixed. Some groups are very organised. They provide excellent services and have in place procedures and structures that cover important issues such as equal opportunities, complaints procedures and quality assurance mechanisms. However, smaller or older organisations may only be beginning to look now at these issues in relation to the contracting requirements of social services departments. However just because policies are not in place does not mean that these issues and concerns are not treated sensitively. We should never run the risk of equating voluntary with amateur. Without the large leaden structures that tie up social services departments, voluntary organisations can bring a degree of flexibility to the delivery of service which we will want to make use of. Sharing confidential information can sometimes be a worry particularly if a voluntary organisation has very local links with the community. If this is a worry it needs to be shared. There may not be problems just because immediate neighbours of the older person are involved in delivering the service. As long as choice is an option within the organisations these problems can usually be overcome. If, of course, we are unhappy with any service, we must speak with the organisation or our line manager and pass this information on to quality assurance units where this is appropriate.

Important others

A wider group than just those we have looked at so far may be involved in any one individual's care. There may, for example, be someone like a sheltered housing warden, or a day care worker involved. Our contact may be less frequent and there may be issues about what information we share. This will be done usually on a need to know basis. However, we need to make sure that these colleagues know where we are and that we can be approached if there seem to be problems or issues that need to be aired. Is there a new problem or is there something they see in the care plan that others have missed? If they are coming new to work with this particular person, they may want to discuss questions about risk or to know more about the other services involved.

Working successfully with others calls for the application of all the usual skills that we put into play in working with older people themselves. This means listening, encouraging and, one that is often forgotten, thanking people for what they do.

The last word

This is not a job for shrinking violets.

Appendix

I Arthritis

Arthritis is a type of rheumatic disease. It is a disease common amongst older people, but not exclusively so. Osteoarthritis is the kind of arthritis most likely to affect older people. It develops gradually, usually over several years and is the result of the cartilage which covers the bone (within the joint) becoming worn and rough. The membrane and capsule surrounding the joint also becomes thicken and inflamed. As a result the joint becomes stiff and painful. If the Osteoarthritis worsens, the cartilage can become so worn away that the bones of the joint begin to rub together. The joints most likely to be affected are knees, hips, feet and hands.

Likely effects

For most people arthritis causes discomfort, stiffness and pain, the consequences of which can lead to a great deal of frustration for the sufferer. It is not uncommon for those with arthritis to sometimes experience periods of depression. Coming to terms with a dependence on others; getting used to the time that must now be taken to wash and dress; having to plan in advance any manoeuvre such as getting in and out of bed or going to the shops, can be very difficult to accept. The degree to which tasks will present this kind of difficulty will depend on the pain and difficulty an individual experiences, the progress of the disease, the efficiency of pain control and the individual's tolerance of the pain.

Treatment

Analgesics (i.e. Paracetamol) can be helpful in relieving pain.

Anti-inflammatory drugs – Naproxen (Naprosyn), Piroxicam (Feldene), Fenbufen (Lederfen), Ibuprofen (Brufen), Indomethacin (Indocid) and others can offer pain relief and help to reduce joint swelling.

Steroids – Cortisone Prednisolone (Prednesol), Betamethasone (Betnovate) are usually used to treat 'flare ups' of the disease.

139

Surgery may be an option if the joints have become very badly damaged. Hips, knees, fingers, shoulders, elbows, ankles and wrists can all be replaced. Hip replacement is by far the most common and the most successful. There is a 95 per cent chance that following a hip replacement an individual will be free from pain and could recover up to three-quarters of the range of normal hip movement. Replaced joints can of course sometimes fail and if this happens they may have to be removed.

Useful equipment

OTs can suggest a very wide range of equipment to help with movement, in the kitchen, the bathroom and in managing personal care. Dressing aids are widely available as is clothing with velcro fastenings, to help make dressing and undressing easier.

Organisations

Arthritis Care is a national voluntary organisation. They have an information service, can sometimes help with grants; they organise over 500 branches which in turn run social activities and offer support. They can run special holiday centres and a residential home. For more information contact them at 18 Stephenson Way, London NW1 2HD, 0171 916 1500. Scotland – Mrs Patricia Wallace 0141 942 2322. Northern Ireland – Mrs Rita Douglas 01232 669 882.

II Dementia

Dementia is not a part of normal ageing but is a progressive disease which affects an individual's memory, perceptions and understanding of their situation. Dementia is more common in people over the age of 80. However it is still a minority disease affecting only ten in 100 of the over 60s population. The types and causes of dementia can vary. Alzheimer's Disease and Multi-infarct dementia are the most common to affect older people, but others such as Lewy Body dementia and Korsakoff's Syndrome (an alcohol-related dementia) are also present in the older population.

Alzheimer's disease damages brain cells causing a progressive deterioration in intellect, social functioning and eventually the ability to manage personal care. Although no hard and fast statements can be made, there is an understanding that, on average, people with this type of dementia will die within four to twelve years from onset of the illness. The effects and progress of the disease will be different for each person. The first symptom is memory loss. People may retain a good long term memory but forget recent events. There may be a loss of understanding in relation to what time or day of the week it is. Some people may forget familiar names and faces. There may be some changes to personality. A women who has previously been quite a reserved person, may begin to lose her inhibitions and become more outspoken. As the disease progresses even the most simple tasks may become difficult to manage and the older person may need help to dress, wash and eat. The changes that begin to take place for the person with dementia require a great deal of understanding on the part of family and friends.

Multi-infarct dementia is the result of small strokes occurring in the brain. These small strokes affect the blood flow, causing individuals to feel unwell or to appear confused for a short period of time. Sometimes these episodes can go unnoticed. The damage done as a result of the strokes will cause changes in the level of function the older person is able to maintain. An individual may have a degree of insight into the problems they are experiencing and, as a consequence, depression may also be a factor. The difficulties a person with Multi-infarct dementia will experience will be very similar to those outlined above. If this type of dementia is diagnosed it is likely that other vascular problems are also present.

Treatment

There is no treatment for dementia, although medication may be used to try and alleviate some of the particular symptoms. For example drugs may be given to reduce anxiety or to help the person to rest and sleep. Such medication can include: Phenothiazine (Merrill), Chlormethiazole (Heminevrine), Dichloraltphenazone (Welldorm). Social and environmental management are the key to making this disease less stressful to all concerned.

Organisations

Alzheimer's Disease Society (England and Wales) Gordon House, 10 Greencoat Lane, London SW1P2 1PH, 0171 306 0606.
Alzheimer Scotland Action on Dementia, 8 Hill Street, Edinburgh EH2 3JZ, 0131 225 1453.
Alzheimer's Disease Society, 11 Wellington Park, Belfast BT9 6DJ, 01232 664 100.

All provide information, can give details of carers groups, some manage and run local home support and day care services.

Reading

Some useful texts are mentioned in the References section.

III Heart problems – some terms and descriptions

Angina – occurs when the heart muscle becomes starved of oxygen. The blood is not getting through to deliver the oxygen to the muscle at the rate needed to meet the demands of the activity being undertaken. The restriction in the flow of blood is normally due to a narrowing of the arteries. Treatment is with drugs. The types used fall into three main groups: (a) Nitrates, i.e. Glyceryl-Trinitrate (GTN, Percutol), Isosorbide Dinitrate (Cedocard, Isordil, Sorbitrate) and Isosorbide Mononitrate (Elantan, Monit); (b) Beta Blockers i.e. Atenolol (Tenormin), Metoprolol (Betaloc), Propranolol (Inderal); (c) Nifedipine (Adalat).

This is not an exclusive or exhaustive list, but examples of the most commonly prescribed drugs.

Arteriosclerosis – term used to describe the narrowing of the arteries.

Atrial fibrillation – means that the heart is beating irregularly, the common cause (although not exclusively) is often coronary heart disease. This condition is usually treated with medication i.e. Lanoxin (Digoxin).

Coronary heart disease – is a degenerative condition, coronary arteries (which supply blood to the heart) become narrow and obstructed. This is caused by a build up of atheroma (fatty deposits) in the affected arteries. The most usual preventive treatment is a change to lifestyle, stopping smoking, taking exercise, eating a balanced diet and, if needed, losing weight.

Coronary Thrombosis – a heart attack caused by inadequate blood supply to the heart. A thrombosis will result in an area of the muscle becoming damaged, leading it to function poorly thereafter.

Embolus – a blood clot.

Heart failure – the lessening in the heart's ability to pump blood effectively around the body, circulation slows and becomes congested. A person may become tired and short of breath, their ankles may swell as they retain fluid. The resulting heart failure may bring pain (Angina) on exertion. Treatment is usually with drugs to steady the heartbeat and increase pumping efficiency. Some of these drugs are mentioned above.

Hypertension – high blood pressure in the arterial circulation, does not present any symptoms, but can be identified if blood pressure is checked.

Ischaemic heart disease – is present where there is a poor blood supply to an area of the heart muscle, so weakening it.

Transient ischaemic attack – mini-stroke, temporary loss of blood to brain similar to a stroke except that full recovery will follow.

Useful organisations

Chest Heart and Stroke Association, CHSA House, Whitecross Street, London EC1Y 8JJ, 0171 490 7999.
CHSA Scotland, 65 North Castle Street, Edinburgh EH2 3LT, 0131 225 6963.
CHSA Northern Ireland, 21 Dublin Road, Belfast BT2 2FJ, 01232 320 184.

Produce information leaflets, can sometimes give grants, have local branches which provide a range of social activities for members.

IV Strokes

A stroke or Cardiovascular Accident (CVA) occurs when the blood supply to part of the brain has suddenly stopped. The area of the brain that is affected dies, the sufferer therefore being left with some degree of disability, the severity of which will depend on the extent of the stroke.

Likely effects

Speech and paralysis are the most common problems to be experienced. If speech is affected an individual may experience Aphasia, that is to have difficulty putting thoughts into words, or Apraxia, difficulty putting words into speech or in putting a sequence of actions together. As someone tries to talk they may slur their speech (Dysarthria) or fix on one word or phrase that is then repeatedly used to describe any action. An individual may have some degree of weakness or loss of use and sensitivity in their limbs, hearing, sight and touch. Some people may have involuntary movement in their limbs and may have difficulty remembering or being able to focus on the affected limb.

Treatment

Intensive physiotherapy will be needed to help return movement to affected limbs. If swallowing is a difficulty a special diet may be required. An individual may also need to get new dentures fitted. Recovery will mean learning new ways of coping with daily tasks. Bladder control may have to be relearned and the individual will have to

144   *Appendix*

learn to work with new aids and equipment. All of this requires a great deal of motivation from the individual and their family.

Equipment

OT departments will have many aids that will be of practical use. These include kitchen utensils, bathing and walking aids. People who have had strokes need to discover Velcro. OTs may also be able to recommend clothing companies who specialise in easy care clothing.

Organisations

Chest Heart and Stroke Association, as mentioned previously.

References

References in this book have been kept to an absolute minimum. This list is not therefore comprehensive in any way. Nevertheless, included in this list are books and articles that we have found to be useful reading. Those marked with an asterisk (*) are particularly recommended as useful additional reading.

Age Concern England (1986) *The Law and Vulnerable Elderly People*, London: Age Concern England.
Age Concern England (1995) *Your Rights*, London: Age Concern England.
Allen, I., Hogg, D. and Peace, S. (1992) *Elderly People: Choice, Participation and Satisfaction*, London: PSI.
Barnet Task Force (1981) *Barnet Pensioners Health Courses*, Barnet Health Education Council.
Bond, M. (1979) 'Women's Work in a Woman's World', MA Dissertation, Warwick University, School for Advanced Urban Studies.
Brearly, P. (1982) *Risk and Ageing: Hazards and Helpings*, London: Routledge & Kegan.
British Geriatric Society (1978) *The Guidelines for Collaboration between Geriatric Physicians and Psychiatrists in the Care of the Elderly*, London: British Geriatric Society.
Brown, P. D. and Siegal, D. L. (1989) *Ourselves Growing Older: Women Ageing with Knowledge and Power*, British Edition by Jean Shapiro, London: Fontana Collins.
Chapman, A. and Marshall, M. (eds) (1994) *Dementia: New Skills for Social Workers* London: Jessica Kingsley.
Clark, D. M. (1991) *Good Neighbours: A Practical Guide to Setting up a Village Care Group*, York: Joseph Rowntree Foundation.
Collins, D. and Basith, A. (1994) *Concise Guide to Customs of Minority Ethnic Religions* London: Ashgate Publishing.
Commission of European Communities (1993) *Age and Attitudes: Main Results from a Barometer Survey.*
Connor, A. and Tibbit, J. (1988) *Social Workers and Health Care in Hospitals*, Social Work Services Group, Edinburgh: HMSO.
Cooper, B. (1988) *Over the Hill: Reflections on Ageism between Women*, California: The Crossing Press.
Cooper, J. D. (1980) *Social Groupwork with Elderly People in Hospital*, Keele: Beth Johnson Foundation, University of Keele.
* Cooper, M., Merdeem, S., Redstone, E., Myers, M., Taylor, D. and

Woolf, A. (Hen House Co-op) (1992) *Growing Old Disgracefully*, London: Piatkus Press.

Department of Health (1994) *Hospital Discharge Handbook: A Manual on Hospital Discharge Practice*, London: DOH.

Department of Health, Social Services Inspectorate and Scottish Office Social Work Services Group (1991) *Care Management and Assessment: Practitioners Guide*, London: HMSO.

Department of Health, Social Services Inspectorate (1993) *Inspecting for Quality: Standards for the Residential Care of Elderly People with Mental Disorders*, London: HMSO.

Ellis, K. (1993) *Squaring the Circle – User and Carer Participation in Needs Assessments*, York: Joseph Rowntree Trust.

Feil, N. (1982) *Validation – the Feil Method*, Ohio: Edward Feil Productions.

Fineman, S. (1985) *Social Work Stress and Intervention*, London: Gower Press.

* Forster, M. (1989) *Have the Men Had Enough*, London: Chatto.

Frogatt, A. (1990) *Family Work with Elderly People*, Practical Social Work Series, London: Macmillan Press.

Gambrill, E. and Stein, T. J. (1983) *Supervision: A Decision Making Approach*, Human Services Guide 35, London: Sage.

Goldberg, E. M., Walker, D. and Robinson, J. (1977) 'Exploring the Task Centred Casework Method', *Social Work Today* 9, 2.

* Gray, B. and Issacs, B. (1979) *Care of the Elderly Mentally Infirm*, London: Tavistock Publications.

* Hudson, B. (1993) *The Busy Person's Guide to Care Management*, Social Services Monographs Research in Practice, Joint Unit for Social Services Research, University of Sheffield and Community Care.

Jacques, A. (1992) *Understanding Dementia* (2nd edn), Edinburgh: Churchill Livingston.

* Lessing, D. (1984) *The Diaries of Jane Somers*, London: Penguin Books.

Lynch, M. A. (1976) 'The Critical Path', *Journal of Maternal and Child Health* 25–9 July.

Macdonald, B. and Rich, C. (1985) *Look Me in the Eye: Old Women, Ageing and Ageism* London: The Women's Press.

Marris, P. (1974) *Loss and Change*, London: Routledge & Kegan Paul.

* Marshall, M. (1990) *Working with Dementia: Guidelines for Professionals*, London: Venture Press.

Mayle, F. (1989) *Dynamic Interviewing: Social Work Methods*, Human Resources Series No. 41, London: Sage.

McEwan, E. (1992) *The Consumer Perception of Need in Long Term Care for Elderly People: Purchasing Providing Quality*, London: Age Concern/HMSO.

* McGahern, J. (1990) *Amongst Women*, London: Faber & Faber.

National Carers Association (1994) *Facts About Carers* (23) What is a Carer? London.

* Neill, J. (1989) *Assessing Elderly People for Residential Care: A Practical Guide*, London: NISW.

Neill, J. and Williams, C. (1992) *Leaving Hospital: Elderly People and their Discharge from Hospital,* London: HMSO.

Norman, A. (1987) *Rights and Risks,* London Centre for Policy on Ageing. Second reprint with revised foreword. First printed 1980.

* Papadopulus, A. (1993) *Counselling Carers,* Bicester: Winslow Press.

Partridge, C. J., Johnston, M. and Morris, L. (1991) *Disability and Health Service Perceptions and Beliefs and Experiences of Old People,* London: King's College.

Pedlar, M. and Boydell, I. (1985) *Managing Yourself,* London: Fontana Press.

Pfeffer, N. and Coote, A. (1993) *Is Quality Good for You? A Critical Review of Quality Assurance in Welfare Services,* London: Policy Studies Institute.

Phillipson, C. (1982) *The Capitalism and Construction of Old Age,* London: Macmillan Press.

Pincus, A. and Minahan, A. (1973) *Social Work Practice: Model and Method,* Washington: Peacock Press.

Pritchard, J. (1992) *The Abuse of Elderly People: A handbook for professionals,* London: Jessica Kingsley.

Royal College of Physicians of London (1994) *Ensuring Equity and Quality of Care for Elderly People,* 'The interface between geriatric medicine and general (internal) medicine, London: Royal College of Physicians.

Scottish Action on Dementia (1990) *Dementia and Money Matters: A Guide for Carers,* Edinburgh: Alzheimer Scotland – Action on Dementia.

Scottish Action on Dementia (1988) *Dementia and the Law: The Challenge Ahead,* Edinburgh: Alzheimer Scotland – Action on Dementia.

Scutton, S. (1992) *'Ageing, Healthy and in Control',* Therapy in Practice, No. 29, London: Chapman & Hall.

Smith, C. R. (1982) *Social Work with the Dying and Bereaved,* London: Macmillan.

Stokes, G. (1988) *Screaming and Shouting,* Bicester: Winslow Press.

* Taylor, B. and Devine, T. (1993) *Assessing Needs and Planning Care in Social Work,* London: Arena Askgate Publishing.

* Toole, Kennedy. J. (1980) *A Confederacy of Dunces,* London: King Penguin.

* Treacy, D. (1991) *Clear Your Desk, The Definitive Guide to Conquering Your Paper Workload – Forever,* London: Business Books.

Victor, C. R. (1991) *Health and Health Care in Later Life,* Milton Keynes: OU Press.

West, S. (1994) *Your Rights: A Guide to Money Benefits for Older People,* London: ACE Books.

Index

abuse 122
access 47
accommodation *see* housing
activities
  in retirement 25
  outside the family 33
  volunteering 35
age of retirement 15
ageism 13, 27–31, 33, 34
aggression 75–6
anti-discriminatory practice 67
area teams 44–6, 48
arthritis 5, 18
assessment 3–5, 41, 46, 78, 85,
  87, 94–9, 104–11
attendance allowance 82

behind the scenes work 52
being alone 14
benefits 77, 82–3
birth rate 9–10
black people 11–12, 48
  see also cultural perceptions
bottom line 77

care management 45, 66, 86–7,
  108–9, 111, 114
care plans *see* care
  management
carers 36–8, 71, 102–3, 108,
  125–6
case conference 106
casework 71
charging 83–4, 106–7, 113
choice 4, 46, 104, 111–12, 114
Chronically Sick and Disabled
  Persons Act 77, 80
communication skills 51, 93–8,
  101–2, 108, 122–3

community care 2, 78, 129
  assessments 46, 49, 60
  legislation 30
community psychiatric
  nurses 50, 98, 133
community support 17
compulsory admission 79
confidentiality 94, 100
costs *see* charging
counselling 71–2
Court of protection 80
co-working 73
crisis intervention 70–1
critical path analysis 73
cultural perceptions 16, 25, 96
curator bonus 80

deafness *see* hearing loss
death 123–5
decision making 13, 63–4, 128
dementia 19, 76, 84, 98–9
demographic changes *see*
  population
depression 19, 93
developing new services 51–2
  see also working together
difficult behaviour 76
DIPSW 5
disability 19, 82–3, 97–8
discharge from hospital 42–4,
  126–7
discrimination 68
disengagement 56–7
district nurses 90, 132
doctors *see* general practitioners
  (GPs)
dynamic interviewing 71–2

emergencies 56

emigration 10
equal opportunities 13
ethnic minority population
    figures 11–12

form filling 61, 82, 113
friends 14

general practitioners
    (GPs) 19–20, 87, 130–4
Geriatricians 135
getting started 52–6
good practice 66
groupwork 69
guidelines – legislation 77

health problems 18–19, 34, 97
Health visitors 135
hearing loss 18
Home help services 129
Hospital
    discharge 42–4, 126–7
    social work teams 41–4, 72
housing 17–18, 20, 49

ill health *see* disability
immigration 10–12
income support 81–3
induction of new staff 40
Information 21, 46, 50, 58, 77,
    103
    collection 48, 57–8, 87–90,
        96, 101
    management 54, 57–8
    systems 49, 57–8
Intimate care 38

Jewish welfare organisations 11

knowledge 5, 76–7, 96–7
    see also information

labelling 33
language 48, 61, 96
legislation 4, 77–8
listening 9
    see also communication skills

living alone 13
location 16, 50–1
long term care 116–18, 120
loss 9, 24, 31, 38, 56, 71, 123–5
low income *see* poverty

making contact 91–3
media images 29
men 19
mental health 19, 98
Mental Health Acts 77, 79
money 14–15, 111
    see also benefits
multidisciplinary teams 42, 51–2,
    90
    see also working together

National Assistance Act 77, 79
National Vocational
    Qualification (NVQ) 5
needs-led assessment *see*
    assessment
NHS and Community Care
    Act 2–3, 46, 78, 80
nursing home care 121–2

observation skills 92, 95
occupational therapy 129–30
old age 15, 24, 26, 29, 32
organisational skills 52–4

packages of care *see* care
    management
paperwork 53–4
pensions 15, 81
phone techniques 51
physical aggression *see*
    aggression
physical dependence 37
planning 30, 32, 55, 112
population 7–8, 11–12, 17
poverty 14–15
    see also money, benefits
power of attorney 80
pre-retirement courses 24
problem solving 45
Provision of services 109–10

Psychiatrists   44, 135

quality assurance   13, 112, 114–15

recording   59–62
referral   86, 88–9
residential care   116–20
resources, creating new ones   58
respite care   37
restraint   76
retirement   16, 23–5
risk   76, 104–6
rural populations   17, 51
   see also location

Scottish Vocational
   Qualifications (SVQ)   5
Section   47   *see* National
   Assistance Act
Seeking help   47
Self-care   74
Service providers   4, 58, 109–10
   development   51–2
shock   76
skills   *see* getting started
smoking   20
social services departments   4, 29, 40, 78, 128
social work
   support   38–9

teams   41; *see also* area teams, hospital social work teams
methods   66–9
stereotyping   27–8
   see also ageism
stress   74–6
supervision   62–4
systems approach   *see* unitary approach

task-centred approach   69
time management   52–5
touch   101
trust, building of   62

unitary approach   69

validation therapy   73
verbal aggression   *see* aggression
visiting   55, 91–2
voluntary agencies   49, 135–6
volunteering   34

welfare rights   *see* benefits
well order persons' clinic   19
women   12–13
work beyond retirement   15, 26
working together   51–2, 89–91, 109–11, 128–38
   see also co-working